SCAMBusters!

SCAMBusters!

MORE THAN 60 WAYS SENIORS

GET SWINDLED AND HOW

THEY CAN PREVENT IT

Ron Smith

Collins
An Imprint of HarperCollinsPublishers

All efforts have been made to ensure the accuracy of the information contained in this book as of the date published. The author and the publisher expressly disclaim responsibility for any adverse effects arising from the use or application of the information contained herein.

HarperCollins books may be purchased for educational, business, or sales promotional use. For information, please write: Special Markets Department, HarperCollins Publishers, 10 East 53rd Street, New York, NY 10022.

FIRST EDITION

Designed by Cassandra J. Pappas

Library of Congress Cataloging-in-Publication Data

Smith, Ron, 1934–
    Scambusters: more than 60 ways seniors get swindled and how they can prevent it / by Ron Smith.—1st ed.
        p. cm.
    Includes index.
    ISBN-13: 978-0-06-112023-7
    ISBN-10: 0-06-112023-5
        1. Fraud—United States—Prevention—Handbooks, manuals, etc. 2. Older people—Crimes against—United States—Prevention—Handbooks, manuals, etc. 3. Swindlers and swindling—United States. I. Title. II. Title: Scambusters.

    HV6697.S64 2006
    362.88—dc22   2006040333

    06 07 08 09 10 PC/WBC/RRD 10 9 8 7 6 5 4 3 2 1

Contents

Preface

First, while this book is dedicated to informing and educating seniors about scams, it is not intended to replace legal or investment advice from licensed professionals. The world is complicated enough without practicing "do it yourself" in matters that require expert attention.

Second, much of this book centers around information available on the Internet. The Internet is a fluid community; Web sites come and go with disquieting regularity, and some of what you find on the Internet is speculative and misleading. I have made every attempt to recommend only Web sites that appear legitimate and useful and long-running. But like everybody else working the Internet, I recognize that things change, and what's golden today is dross tomorrow. Plus the fact that I, too, am fallible (yes, folks, I do make occasional mistakes). So whatever you do—and I can't emphasize this enough—*check and double-check any information source before you make a decision affecting your health or your pocketbook.*

Finally, my purpose in writing this book is to show you how to look out for scams so that you'll feel comfortable exploring the Internet and other sources on your own. Awareness is the first line of defense against scams.

Acknowledgments

I would like to thank and dedicate this book to the many seniors who took the time to tell me their experiences, thoughts, and ideas on scams. I would also like to thank my editor at HarperCollins, Ryu Spaeth, for his valuable insights.

SCAMBusters!

Think You Can't Be Scammed?
Take This Test and Find Out

How well prepared are you to avoid common scams, the kind that you pay for in the currency of money and grief? Think you're doing all right? Well, let's find out. Take this short nine-question true-or-false test to see how vulnerable you are to attack from everyday scammers. At the end of the test, score yourself according to the Scam-Savvy Scale.

1. Boomers, followed by seniors, is the demographic group most commonly targeted for scams because they have the largest concentration of money and material possessions, a prime attraction for scammers.
2. Low-to-moderate use of ATM machines lessens one's chances of being robbed or scammed.
3. The homes of affluent people are the usual choice of burglars to ply their craft because that's where the money is.
4. With all the problems associated with online identity theft,

it's much safer to bank in person or by mail and receive your cancelled checks and bank statements by mail.

5. Variable annuities are one of the worst investments seniors can make.

6. In this age of uncertainty when anything can go wrong, from disrupted travel plans to terrorist attacks, as much insurance as you can afford is a necessity.

7. Because hackers and identity thieves constantly roam the Internet, you need to minimize your time online.

8. When selling anything from an old set of golf clubs to your car, accept nothing less than cash, and failing that, certified checks or money orders.

9. Although there is a charge associated with it, an unlisted telephone number is one of the few methods available to disguise your telephone number from crank callers and telemarketers.

Hey, you having fun? Okay, now check the answers below:

1. **False.** The demographic group most commonly targeted for scams is seniors. There are five reasons. Read about them in "Sooner or Later You're Going to Get Scammed" (page 6).

2. **False.** Low-to-moderate use still unduly exposes you to the insidious devices of scammers who will empty your bank account faster than a hungry robin swallowing a worm. Try not to use ATMs except in cases of emergency. Find out more in "ATM Machines" page 12.

3. **False.** The way the statement reads is deceptive (and, I must admit, tricky). It disguises the fact that seniors are frequently

burglarized because they're perceived as people with a great deal of wealth and the easiest marks. Read "Casing Your Home" (page 44).

4. **False.** It's a matter of the lesser of two evils. The most frequently used method to steal your bank account numbers is from bank statements sitting in your exposed mailbox. Banking online is safer if you follow a few basic rules. See "Banking Online" (page 21).

5. **True.** Consumer writer Jane Bryant Quinn says variable annuities are products she "dreams of blowing to smithereens." Find out why in "Variable Annuities" (page 141).

6. **False.** It depends on the type of insurance. Some kinds are needed, others are unnecessary. Go to "Unnneeded Insurance Policies" (page 92) and learn the difference.

7. **False.** There are better ways to prevent hacker intrusions on the information superhighway[1] without curtailing your time online. Find out what they are in "Bogus Web Sites" (page 102), "Dangerous Spam E-mail" (page 105), and "Phishing for Your Credit Card Number" (page 110).

8. **False.** You can't accept even certified checks or money orders at face value because counterfeiters know how to make fakes practically indistinguishable from the real thing. Find out how to make sure you don't get snookered. Read "Money Orders" (page 39).

9. **False.** Your unlisted telephone number, for which you pay a premium fee, is for sale on the Internet. Discover how to prevent unwanted telephone calls using a technique that

---

[1]Another name for the Internet.

won't cost you a nickel. Read "Unlisted Telephone Number" (page 207).

Okay, now add up the number of questions you got right and multiply that by ten. That's your Scam-Savvy Score. Check your score against the scale shown below to see how really and truly adept you are at avoiding scams.

The Scam-Savvy Scale

If your Scam-Savvy Score is in this range:	Here's how good you are at avoiding scams	And here's what you should do about it
90	You're dead-on perfect.	Help me write the next book on scams.
70–80	Up to 20% of the scams working against you are going to be successful. Not good.	Read this book and follow its advice.
50–60	You're about average, which means you're going to get scammed frequently.	Carry this book with you wherever you go and refer to it often.
40 and under	You have much to learn.	Pack your bags and leave town before the next scammer spots you.

All kidding aside, if you scored sixty or below, this book is really going to be an eye-opener, one that may save you many dollars that otherwise would be lost to scammers, not to mention being spared tons and tons of headaches.

If you scored eighty or ninety, it shows you're on the right track, but can still improve your ability to thwart those dastardly scammers. So, read on.

Sooner or Later You're Going to Get Scammed

Allow me to introduce myself. My name is Ron Smith. I'm a senior in my early seventies who's been there, done that. So I understand your problems, your anxieties, and your vulnerabilities. But just so there's no misunderstanding, I'm not a heath-care professional, a financial advisor, an insurance agent, a lawyer, or a priest. What I do is expose scams against seniors. That's why I'm called the Scam Doctor.

The purpose of this book is to alert seniors like you to the more common scams perpetrated on older people. Each of the sections of the book describes a scam, shows how to spot it in action before the scam artist reaches a hand deep inside your pocketbook, and explains how to prevent it from happening in the first place.

As a senior, you're a target, a big, juicy one. The kind that makes scam artists salivate. When they see you coming, they're ready to concoct any number of nefarious schemes to defraud you and rob you of your hard-earned money. It's an unconscionable act, but who ever claimed scam artists are highly moral people?

There are several reasons crooks consider you easy pickings. First, you're part of the fastest-growing demographic age segment, so just on numbers alone it falls to reason you're going to be increasingly targeted. According to the 2000 census, there are 45 million people age sixty and older living in the good old USA.

Second, compared to other age groups, seniors are perceived, rightly or wrongly, as the group that has piles of money: pensions, paid-up annuities, bank certificates of deposit, savings bonds, stocks, corporate bonds, treasury bonds, mutual funds, cash. Just sitting there ripe for the picking, enough to excite any scammer. There's some truth to this belief; this generation of retired Americans, as a whole, is the most affluent in history. Still, there are exceptions. Many seniors have not been fortunate enough to share in the wealth.

Third, you're slowing down. It's a proven fact your brain does not respond as swiftly as it did when you were thirty. A perfect scenario for fast-talking, quick-thinking swindlers working a scam.

Fourth, many of you live alone. Your spouses may have passed on, your children and grandchildren have moved away. You have nobody to help you make decisions that affect your pocketbook. You're on your own, and don't the scammers out there know it.

Fifth, too many of you are not connected to the Internet. Well, shame on you. Scammers are aware of that fact, and they're counting on you remaining in the dark. They realize, better than anyone, how their scams are exposed on literally hundreds of Web sites. And believe me, what scammers fear most is that more and more of you will get connected, thereby exposing their cheating ways. They understand, better than most, that knowledge is power, and there is no greater source of knowledge than what you will find on the information superhighway.

The Internet is a thousand libraries rolled into one. On our subject alone, it describes scams, scam artists, and steps to prevent scams in rich detail. If you don't understand how to use this rich resource, ask for lessons at your library or local senior center. Tapping into the Internet is easier than it appears. Get connected! should be your mantra.

Sooner or later, you're going to get scammed. It's as inevitable as politicians scooping campaign money into their deep pockets. I know about getting scammed because the best in the game have attempted to scam me, and have occasionally succeeded. As a senior I learned the hard way to remain alert and to suspect people I didn't know and question their motives. For two of my most memorable encounters with scam artists, read the "Laser Eye Clinics" section and Appendix A: "Five Rules Seniors Should Follow to Avoid Investment Scams." Both describe personal experiences I've had with these weasels.

Obviously, I can't depict every scam imaginable. To do so would fill a book the size of an unabridged dictionary. What I've done is highlight certain examples that should help you avoid related classes of scams. For example, the topics "Mutual Funds" (page 133), "Variable Annuities" (page 141), and "Financial Planners" (page 114) should alert you to similar types of investment scams. Just follow the principles described in those topics and others in the Investments and Home Ownership section.

One other word before you begin. This book will empower you with the knowledge that helps minimize, even prevent, scams against you, but you need a framework to support that knowledge. Follow these simple ground rules and the framework is yours:

- Stay alert to your surroundings.
- When strangers approach you for any reason, no matter how nice they appear, be wary.

- Don't believe everything you read and hear. Question anything that sounds too good to be true. It pays to be skeptical until proven otherwise.
- Stay calm and remain poised. You have the mental faculties to know the difference between what's good and what's bad for you. Before you make a decision, think it out. Don't panic; investigate.
- Above all, follow your intuition. When something smells bad, it probably is.

That's it. Good luck on your journey. May the gods smile favorably upon you, and after reading this book, may you never be scammed again.

Banking and Credit

It's strange that men should take up crime when there are so many legal ways to be dishonest.

—DR. LAURENCE J. PETER

Scammers are continually aiming at emptying your bank account, filching your credit cards, and stealing your identity. Some world we live in, huh? You have the choice of either neutralizing their deceptive attempts or surrendering and allowing the crooks to have their way. I know you're not going to let them get the best of you; otherwise you wouldn't be reading this book. The topics in this section describe how to protect yourself against common scams in the banking and credit arena, and in the process defeat the weasels who are trying to scam you.

ATM Machines

THE SCAM

You're doing your weekly grocery shopping at the supermarket. You're in the habit of withdrawing money from the ATM machine near the entrance to the store before you begin shopping. You wait a respectful distance from the ATM until the person using it departs, then it's your turn. You have always been careful around ATMs, knowing that it's a place ripe for theft and scams.

You walk up to the ATM and enter your card and your PIN code, every now and then glancing around to your left as the next person on line jiggles his foot impatiently, distracting your attention. What you don't see is the man in back of you on the right using a miniature digital camcorder to record your PIN code from behind a high stack of empty vegetable cartons. When you leave the store after shopping,

> Use ATM machines for cash emergencies exclusively, and then only during daylight hours. High-tech scammers know too many ways to steal your ATM and PIN numbers, and will empty your bank account.

somebody snatches your purse. Thieves now have both your ATM card and PIN code. Within a half hour they've drained your bank account from another ATM.

In another scenario, you approach the ATM and cautiously enter your card and PIN code to withdraw $100. Nobody is around and you feel safe. Still, something is wrong, but you can't quite put your finger on it. You blame it on nerves and make your withdrawal.

Your instincts are operating in high gear; you should have listened to them. What you don't know is that you've been skimmed. Skimming is what happens when thieves place an electronic card-swipe device over the bank's ATM entry slot. The skimmer has been cleverly constructed to look like an integral part of the ATM—same color, same style. The device reads the information on your ATM card. A tiny digital camera mounted in the skimmer itself records your PIN code. A half hour later your bank account has been drained. You've been scammed.

HOW TO SPOT THE SCAM

My wife and I are seniors like you, and what we try to do is avoid ATM machines as much as possible. Since the supermarket where we live has a branch of our bank, we cash a check before grocery shopping or we pay our grocery bill from cash my wife or I have in our pockets. Not that we don't use an ATM, but we use it only occasionally, and only during daylight hours and only if we need emergency cash. Then, first thing the next morning, my wife or I call the bank and check on any unauthorized ATM withdrawals from the day before. Just being cautious, but caution where ATMs are concerned pays dividends.

The problem is that scammers have become so technically

proficient, some even buy their own ATMs to capture your personal banking data, then send your numbers overseas where their counterparts in crime manufacture fake debit and credit cards using your name.

This is very difficult to spot. But you can take a few precautions to reduce the likelihood of losing your ATM information to thieves, as shown below.

HOW TO PREVENT THE SCAM

- First and most important, try to minimize your use of ATMs. If you plan well enough ahead, you can have the cash in your pocket needed to pay for daily purchases. After all, what did you do before ATMs were invented? ATMs are a convenience; just don't become dependent on them. It's simply too risky and becoming riskier every day, as clever thieves develop new ATM technology to rob you of your hard-earned money.
- Second, try never to make a withdrawal from an ATM at night; that's the time you're most likely to be physically assaulted by a robber, or worse.
- Third, anytime you approach an ATM, if something doesn't appear quite right, it could be your instincts kicking into high gear. For example, there might be a new attachment on the ATM that wasn't there the last time you used the machine. Or a sign says "No Tampering," or the ATM looks brand new. Until you check with your bank to make sure its bankers know about the new equipment or new attachment or are aware of the sign, don't use it.
- Fourth, be especially vigilant when an ATM is jammed and there's another ATM next to it, beckoning for your use. That

second ATM could belong to thieves or it could have a skimmer attachment.

- Fifth, never, never give your PIN code to anyone—repeat—anyone.
- Sixth, when you're using an ATM, use one hand to shade the keyboard so any snoops with video cameras or binoculars can't see the PIN code you're punching in.
- Seventh, do not write your PIN code on the ATM card. You're just making it easier for thieves to drain your bank account if they steal your purse or wallet.
- Eighth, within a day after each visit to an ATM (hopefully there won't be many visits), check your account for withdrawals you didn't make, just to be sure. Report any shortages or card loss to the bank immediately to reduce your liability.
- Ninth, if at all possible, use an ATM located within the bank itself where it's under the watchful eyes of bank officers and tellers.

If you lose your ATM card or if it's stolen, and you report it before it's used, you are not responsible for any unauthorized withdrawals. If you report it missing within two days, your liability is limited to $50. If you report it missing between two days and sixty days, your liability is $500. If you do not report it missing within sixty days of the receipt of your bank statement, you could lose your entire bank account.

Needless to say, time is of the essence.

Fraudulent Withdrawals

THE SCAM

You receive a call from your bank informing you that your checking account is grossly overdrawn, and that the bank has deducted a substantial amount of money from your savings account to cover the shortfall.

Frantically you search through your bankbook but cannot find any check you have written that would result in an overdrawn account. By your calculations you have a surplus in your checking account.

Further investigation with the bank reveals that a third party has been raiding your account with electronic withdrawals and writing checks on your account around town to pay for upscale merchandise.

Despite their professionally installed computer systems, banks make mistakes, too. Balance your bankbook every month and report errors promptly to the bank to minimize your liability.

You know you've taken every precaution to assure scam artists can't access your personal information such as checking account number, check routing number, Social Security number, and driver's license number.

So what's going on?

HOW TO SPOT THE SCAM

Regardless of how careful you are, there is always the possibility that identity thieves will find a new way to unearth your personal information. But the chances are slim if you follow the suggestions contained in this book. Assuming you do, then in this instance you must conclude that the bank somehow got careless. It could be something like not shredding checks and documents, inadequate internal banking procedures, insufficient attention to vital checks and balances, or poor employee training—some mistake that allowed thieves to glom onto your identity. You read about this kind of thing in the newspapers or see it almost every week on TV.

HOW TO PREVENT THE SCAM

- Knowing that bank errors do occur, the onus is on you to check and verify your bank accounts on a timely basis. If you bank online, you can track your accounts daily, thereby putting yourself in position to catch the first bogus withdrawal before much damage is done. You are now prepared to stop the bleeding before it erupts into a hemorrhage.
- Many online banks have a system that will e-mail you every time a check is written against your account and every time a deposit is made, if you so wish. All you have to do is open your e-mail daily to verify that your bank account isn't being raided.

- If you don't bank online, reconcile your bank statement and balance your account every month. This system is somewhat after the fact, but it's better than nothing. By federal law, if you file a complaint with the bank within sixty days of the fraud, you won't lose a penny provided you've acted responsibly; the bank is then obligated to reimburse you in full.

The words "acted responsibly" denotes specific actions you must take to prevent fraud. In addition to the steps described above, The National Check Fraud Center (http://www.ckfraud.org) advises the following:

- Order your checks through the bank and not from some separate company where identity theft controls may not be as stringent. Banks incorporate measures in their checks to detect counterfeiting.
- When you receive new checks, verify that you have them all. If one or more are missing, contact the bank immediately and put a stop order on the missing check numbers.
- At home, keep checks, bank statements, and cancelled checks in a locked and secure place. Don't leave your checkbook in the car.
- When writing checks:
  - Write with dark ink that can't be erased or written over.
  - Don't leave blank spaces anywhere on the check. Fill in *every* space. On the bottom left-hand corner, write in the reason for the check (purchase shoes, lawn service, etc.).
  - Don't write a check for cash unless you do so at the bank and you're cashing it yourself. Anybody, including a thief, can cash it.

- If you don't bank online, drop off bills at the post office or that familiar blue U.S. Postal Service mailbox. Do not place bills in your mailbox for the postman to pick up. Thieves may get there first, alter your checks, and use them to go on a buying spree.

- Under no circumstances reveal your bank account number over the phone. This is a popular ruse that scam artists use when they want to raid your bank account. Be wary of anybody asking for that information anywhere. For example, a clerk in a store has no business asking for or knowing your bank account number.

- When you've completed your tax return, destroy your old bank statements, cancelled checks, and ATM receipts. After preparing my income tax, I burn everything; it's the safest way. Until then, any paper containing sensitive information stays locked up and hidden.

- Regardless of who asks that you write your Social Security number on your check, refuse to do it. It's not required to write a legitimate check or endorse one. If somebody insists, complain to the manager. Or cancel the transaction and walk away.

- Endorse a check made out to you only at the moment of depositing the check or cashing it. If it's lost or stolen and you've already endorsed it, thieves will be able to cash it.

- Cashier's checks can be counterfeited; they're the latest scam that con artists use to lure unsuspecting seniors. If somebody you don't know offers you a cashier's check in a transaction, have that person accompany you to the bank to verify its authenticity. If the cashier's check is from a distant location, especially from overseas, do not complete your part of the transaction until the check has cleared and the money has been deposited in your account.

ALSO SEE: "Banking Online" (page 21) and "Identity Theft" (page 31).

Banking Online

THE SCAM

There's nothing wrong with banking online. In fact, it prevents thieves from stealing bank statements from your mailbox, a disaster-in-waiting that can gain thieves access to your bank account.

The problem with banking online is when a hacker identity thief plants software called a keylogger on your computer's hard drive. That device records your keystrokes and transmits them to the identity thief, thereby allowing him access to your online bank account sign-in name and password. Not good news.

> By banking online you're less vulnerable to scams. The most common form of identity theft today is stealing bank statements from mailboxes. With online banking your statements stay online, not in your mailbox.

But banks are now countering the ploy. Bank of America, for example, offers what it calls MySiteKey, an additional identification step using an image, a message, and three confirmation answers to questions only you can know. It helps you recognize that you're at a valid Bank of America Web site and not in the hands of a thief's bogus Web site.

HOW TO SPOT THE SCAM

The best way is to check your bank balances on a timely basis. I check mine weekly, sometimes daily. It's quick and easy to do if you bank online, and enables you to spot a withdrawal you didn't authorize. You're now in a position to freeze your bank accounts before too much damage has been done.

If you don't bank online, it's almost impossible to call the bank daily, even weekly, and ask a bank clerk to run your account through the computer to detect unauthorized withdrawals. It can be done, but if too many seniors ask for this service, before you know it, you'll be charged a fee or told to take a hike. Best bet is to bank online. (C'mon, you can do it. Get over your fear; it's really and truly easy—and fun. Your friendly local banker will show you how.)

HOW TO PREVENT THE SCAM

- First, I advise using a dial-up account to gain access to the Internet when you bank online. With broadband, you stay connected to the Internet whether or not you're online. With dial-up, your exposure is limited to the time you're online, thereby significantly reducing the opportunities for hacker identity thieves to strike.[2]

[2]Someday, probably within the near future, I'm certain broadband surfing will be just as safe as dial-up. But not right now.

- Next, make sure you sign off from the online bank when you've completed your business. Not signing off and remaining online at some other Web site leaves your account open and accessible to hackers.

- Third, get a firewall for your computer. It's beyond the scope of this book to discuss the intricacies of firewall protection. Just remember that a firewall protects you from intrusions. Today, it's a necessary component to prevent hackers from gaining access to your hard drive where all your personal information is stored. One such firewall is Zone Alarm. It's available free as a download through *PC* magazine. Visit http://www.pcmag.com, click on the download section, then type "zone alarm" in the search box and click the button. You'll be taken to a section showing you how to download the firewall software. (For alternative Web sites that have firewall downloads, see "*PC (Hard Drive) Firewall Protection*" in Appendix B: Helpful Resources.

- Fourth, passwords are often difficult to recall, so you may need to store them and have them available for reference. One caveat: do not store them either online or on your computer. Clever hackers can find ways to harvest that information. I store mine on two computer disks, the second as a backup to the first. That way they're always accessible, yet out of harm's way.

- Fifth, think twice about downloading anything "free" on the Internet, such as screensavers or comic-book cursors. They may look colorful and appeal to your senses, but they also might contain keyloggers. At the very least they could allow marketers to track your online journey, which opens the door to spam e-mail, the online equivalent of junk mail.

ALSO SEE: *"Fraudulent Withdrawals" (page 16); "Identity Theft" (page 31); "Bogus Web Sites" (page 102); "Dangerous Spam E-mail" (page 105); "Phishing for Your Credit Card Number" (page 110); "Investment Schemes" (page 125).*

Credit Counseling Services

THE SCAM

Like many seniors, you may be in debt. You have little cash left in the bank and you've maxed out your credit cards. You're desperate for help. You turn to one of the many advertised credit counseling services. A very kind young lady assures you that she'll negotiate with your creditors, and with her help you'll get out of debt. She claims her organization has talked creditors into reducing the debt of hundreds of other seniors. You have faith in her and her counseling service because, like all credit counseling services, the organization she works for is allowed a non-profit status by the IRS. That recognition lends her organization a veneer of respectability. It assures you.

> If you're a senior struggling to pay bills, credit counselors can help. But if any require fees, back away. Legitimate credit counselors are paid by creditors.

She signs you up for a debt-management plan that allows her to siphon off your remaining cash from the bank for payment of her fee. The woman never once approaches your creditors. Before you realize what's hit you, your creditors have referred your case to bill collectors and they start hounding you day and night. You're knocking on the door of bankruptcy. The credit counseling service was a scam.

HOW TO SPOT THE SCAM

A legitimate credit counseling service helps you by showing you how to budget your money. It has no authority to bargain with creditors to knock off portions of your debt, though it will work with them to restructure lower payments. You then send monthly payments to the credit counseling service, which forwards the money to your creditors. If a credit counseling service tells you it can talk creditors into reducing your debt, drop it like a sack of hot coals and move to the next one—before you've paid out any fees, of course.

Speaking of fees, a legitimate credit counseling service won't charge you fees because it obtains payment for its services from your creditors. If it asks for money, that's another warning sign of an impending scam.

Some credit counseling services will claim to clear up black marks on your credit record, including bankruptcy filings or foreclosures, by negotiating with the three major credit bureaus. That's an outright lie. Furthermore, it's illegal for a credit counseling service to claim it can. If a credit counseling service makes that claim, report it to the local Better Business Bureau (BBB), or notify the Federal Trade Commission (www.ftc.gov). Call the FTC toll-free at 1-877-FTC-HELP (1-877-382-4357).

HOW TO PREVENT THE SCAM

- Go online to the National Federation for Credit Counseling (http://www.nfcc.org) to find legitimate credit counseling services. Or call that organization toll-free at 1-800-388-2227. It will help you identify a few services that may be right for you, close to where you live. And it won't charge for its advice and suggestions.

- Talk with your creditors to narrow down your selection of a credit counseling service. Ask them if they recommend one that is effective and fair. They'll steer you in the right direction. And they'll most assuredly steer you away from fraudulent organizations.

- Whatever credit counselor you select, make sure you fully understand the services provided, its costs to you, if any (there shouldn't be anything over a token amount for processing your paperwork), and how long the process will take.

- After you've made a decision, contact the Better Business Bureau (http://www.bbb.com) to see if complaints have been filed against the credit counseling service. A string of complaints is an indication of trouble.

- Review the credit counseling contract before you sign. If possible, get help from a lawyer or another professional who understands contracts.

ALSO SEE: "Identity Theft" (page 31).

Debit Cards

THE SCAM

You're a senior who has been careful to own no more than one credit card. Your credit rating is good. You've never had any credit problems or disputes with merchants.

Recently your credit card company issued you a debit card. Hey, this is great, you think. Another convenient way to pay for goods and services without hassles. You start using the debit card without incident, until one day you buy a cashmere sweater from a discount store's closeout sale. After taking it home, you notice a tear in the fabric. You bring the sweater back to the store for an exchange, but the item has been discontinued and there are no replacements. The store wants to give you a credit slip for the purchase price. You tell the manager you don't want credit, you want a refund. The argument goes on for six weeks. You have to threaten

> **D**ebit cards are the worst choice for seniors compared to cash and credit cards. They are fraught with problems and make it relatively easy for scammers to defraud you, and empty your bank account.

a lawsuit before the store reluctantly hands your money back. You don't need the stress this event has produced.

Or, in another scenario, you buy three DVDs online using your debit card, and are astonished to discover recurring charges as the online store mails you three additional DVDs the following month. DVDs you didn't order. Sure, the law protects you from this scam, but you may have to wait months and write many letters and fill out many forms with the merchant, your bank, and law enforcement agencies before you see the first dollar of your money back. The hassle is enough to send you to your doctor complaining of stomach pains.

HOW TO SPOT THE SCAM

When you use a debit card, the amount is automatically and immediately withdrawn from your bank account. If something goes wrong with the purchase, your leverage against the merchant has been reduced considerably. The store's already got your money, and now you have to get it back. That's not a good position to be in.

In a credit card purchase, assuming you dispute the charge before you pay your credit card bill, the merchant is more likely to make some accommodation with you to receive payment. You have control.

HOW TO PREVENT THE SCAM

The problems associated with debit cards, difficult enough for younger people to handle, are especially onerous for senior citizens who have health issues such as depression and stress associated with age. You can take steps to either prevent debit card scams or minimize their potential for problems:

- You have the choice to either use debit cards or not use them. They have too many problems at this stage of their development (which I'm sure, given time, will be resolved). Until then, my advice is to use cash and credit cards.
- If you choose to use debit cards, under the law you have some protection if they're lost or stolen, but those protections are not as strong as they are for credit cards:
  - Your liability is $50 if you notify the bank within two days of the theft or loss.
  - From three days to sixty days, you may be on the hook for unauthorized charges up to $500.
  - Wait more than sixty days and you could lose everything you have in your bank account, including overdraft protection.
  - For the present time, the banking industry has voluntarily capped all losses at $50, but who knows if this will last? There is no law requiring banks to do so.
- If you must use debit cards, confine their use to small, routine purchases such as groceries and gas. But remember to deduct the amounts from your checkbook, and do so at the time of purchase or within minutes of making your purchases so you don't forget.
- Do not use debit cards to make purchases by telephone or online. Problem resolution is much more difficult if you don't have face-to-face access to merchants.

Identity Theft

THE SCAM

It happens every day: clever scam artists manage to steal your identity, then use it to get credit cards and loans, and purchase cars and jewelry. Others will gladly use your identity to launder money, defraud the IRS, and ship money out of the country. And guess who the authorities flock to first?

> Identity theft is the fastest growing crime in the USA. If somebody steals your identity, it will take at least a year with a lot of hassles to clear your name.

You guessed it: you. It's then incumbent upon you to clear your name. And that can be an enormous headache.

HOW TO SPOT THE SCAM

There are many ways, none of them good. Here are some examples: You discover thieves have been using your credit card to buy a mink coat; the Feds try to arrest you on charges of income tax evasion and money laundering; you stop receiving mail because identity thieves have forwarded your mail to their address; and the Social Security Administration accuses you of attempting to open another account under your name. All these traumas and more will snarl you in paperwork, heartache, and tears of frustration for a year or so.

HOW TO PREVENT THE SCAM

There are some very effective ways to defeat this scam:

- One of the more common methods of identity theft is stealing mail from home mailboxes. If possible, try to receive mail at a post office box, or failing that, at a box rented from one of the commercial mail companies such as Pak Mail or Mailboxes Etc. They offer the best security for sensitive mail that contains personal identification, such as a driver's license renewal.
- Do not place your name on the mailbox. A street name and number is sufficient. Why make it easier for identity thieves? Once they have both your name and address, all they need is one other critical piece of information to steal your identity, such as your Social Security number or your checking account routing number.
- Always drop outgoing mail at the post office or in those friendly blue U.S. postal boxes. Don't leave outgoing mail in your mailbox (unless it has a lock on it) and expect it never to be stolen.
- Don't carry around your Social Security card, Medicare card, or any other card that contains sensitive information. As a

senior you're a tempting target for pickpockets, robbers, and purse snatchers. I realize this step is a pain in the neck, but it may prevent your identity from being stolen.

- Minimize the number of credit cards you carry.
- Don't freely hand over your Social Security number to a cashier at Wal-Mart or some other store when she asks for identification. You're not required to do so. Show her some other form of identification. And when you go to the doctor's office, don't surrender your Social Security number there either; they're notorious for requesting unneeded information. Your Social Security number will be required to establish a bank or brokerage account, but not in most other instances.
- At no time should you recite sensitive information like a credit card number over the telephone unless you're *absolutely sure* of the source. I try to avoid doing this simply because you never really know whom you're talking to on the other end of the line. Clever identity thieves have been known to represent themselves as members of organizations you know, such as your bank or credit card company. And remember, legitimate organizations don't solicit sensitive information over the telephone.
- Get a copy of your credit report at least annually from all three credit reporting agencies:
  - Equifax 1-800-685-1111 (http://www.equifax.com)
  - Experian 1-888-397-3742 (http://www.experian.com)
  - TransUnion 1-800-888-4213 (http://www.transunion.com)
- Should you find information on your credit report you wish to challenge, contact all three of the credit rating agencies as well as the merchant that provided the information to them.

- A smart policy would be to obtain a credit report once every four months from one of the three agencies. That way, you can spot discrepancies on a timely basis. You can also obtain daily updates if someone attempts to apply for credit in your name, through a fee-paid service like www. PrivacyGuard.com. Call toll-free 1-866-GuardMe (1-877-202-8828).

- Follow the advice given in the sections of this book dealing with the Internet.

- Balance your checking account monthly and keep close watch on all your financial transactions. Report discrepancies immediately to your bank or brokerage company.

- Keep copies of your credit card receipts and match them against your credit card statements every month.

- When you discard old bank statements, credit card receipts, cancelled checks, brokerage account statements, and the like, either shred or burn them. Call me paranoid, but I burn everything that contains sensitive information when I'm done with it. That way I'm sure identity thieves can't rifle through my garbage and piece together information they can use to scam me.

- If you receive offers of pre-approved credit or convenience checks from credit card companies, shred the letters and opt out of the consumer credit reporting industry's marketing lists by calling 1-888-567-8688. Otherwise, adept scammers may find the applications and apply for credit cards in your name.

- Finally, store sensitive information in a secure place in your home where thieves would never think of looking. Do not store them in places where they're most likely to look: on the

Internet (Yahoo! Briefcase, for example), on your computer, or on computer disks (unless you hide the disks).

ALSO SEE: "Fraudulent Withdrawals" (page 16); "Banking Online" (page 21); "Credit Counseling Services" (page 25); "Bogus Web Sites" (page 102); "Dangerous Spam E-mail" (page 105); "Phishing for Your Credit Card Number" (page 110).

Interest Loan Checks

THE SCAM

You open your mailbox and find one lonely letter. It's addressed to you with the words "Open Immediately: Valuable Check Inside" printed on the envelope in large red letters. You open the letter and find a check made out to you in the amount of $2,000 from a bank called CitysBanke. Wow, you've heard of CitysBanke. Or is it Citibank? Hey, what's the difference? Must be the same outfit.

You catch your breath and thank the Good Lord because the money couldn't have come at a better time. With the constant increases in drug costs and Medicare and supplemental health insurance premiums, you're a little short on cash. This is a dream come true.

> Never deposit a promotional check you receive in the mail from a so-called lending institution. You could find yourself saddled with a loan you didn't ask for, at a whopping 30 percent interest rate.

The accompanying letter proudly proclaims that your top credit rating entitles you to an instant loan of $2,000 with *no further approval required.* You rush down to the bank and deposit the check. You now have an extra two grand, and won't it come in handy?

What you don't know is that you've just signed up for a loan with an interest rate of 29 percent. And not with Citibank; it's with CitysBanke, a shady loan shark outfit with a name dressed up to resemble a legitimate banking institution. When the payment comes due, you feel like a character in the HBO show *The Sopranos* who's been foolish enough to borrow money from the Mob. Now it's payback time. Pay up or else!

HOW TO SPOT THE SCAM

As a rule, loans from legitimate banks and lending institutions don't come in the mail. Stop right there and do not deposit the check before investigating further. *Depositing it means you've accepted the loan.* As soon as that money finds its way to your account, you're legally on the hook because the letter's fine print, which you didn't bother to read, clearly specifies that deposit of the check is how you agree to the offer.

HOW TO PREVENT THE SCAM

Most phony offers and scams fall away in the harsh light of day with a few probing questions. Clark Howard, consumer reporter, advises the following on his Web site, clarkhoward.com:

- Is the offer from a legitimate bank or lender? You can find out quickly enough by bringing the letter to your local bank and asking the banking officer. She has the sources to determine if the lender you're inquiring about is solid (and it probably isn't).

- Check online. Type in the name of the lender in Yahoo! Search or Google and sit back and watch the Web site addresses unfold. You might consider typing in the word "scam" after the name of the lender and see what that brings up on the screen. One of the great aspects of the Internet is that it involves a gigantic community, literally hundreds of millions of people. So if the loan is a scam, chances are other people have been stung, and they may complain about it in a blog[3] or newsgroup.[4]

- As a third alternative, when you see the letter in your mailbox, remove it, shred the letter or burn it, and drop it in the garbage where it belongs.

[3]An online diary of sorts where the author gets to express his or her opinion on any subject imaginable. "Blog" stands for "Web log."

[4]Online communities revolving around common topics. If you're an RV enthusiast, for example, there will be newsgroups devoted exclusively to RVs. There may be literally thousands of members in a group.

Money Orders

THE SCAM

You're a retired woman in your early sixties. As a profitable diversion you sew frilly white garter belts that brides wear under their wedding dresses, and you sell them for a nice piece of change. Your hubby keeps the books and packages and ships the garter belts. Things are going ahead swimmingly, when one day you receive the largest order for garter belts you've ever had. This order comes from Romania; not your first overseas order, but the first from Eastern Europe. Once you've filled this order you won't have to sew for a couple of months and, frankly, you can use the break since business has been much brisker than anticipated.

When the Romanian buyer mailed you the garter belt order, he sent a large money order to cover your selling price and ship-

> Anytime somebody sends you a money order for a sum greater than the product or service you're offering, and requests that you remit the difference, chances are the money order is a fake.

ping costs because you don't make garter belts to order without money in hand. You look over the money order; it appears genuine.

But the money order is for more than your price, about three hundred dollars more. You e-mail the buyer and he instructs you to wire him the difference. Your hubby takes one look at this and says, Whoa, Nelly, let's check this out. He brings the money order to the post office and asks the postmaster to verify its authenticity. The postmaster examines the money order and declares it a fake. To make sure, he checks the money order's serial number. Its number doesn't show up on the register. The money order is counterfeit. Your husband's caution has saved both of you a lot of time and money.

HOW TO SPOT THE SCAM

It's getting harder and harder to spot phony money orders, so don't try to validate them yourself; it takes an expert. You should be automatically suspicious when you receive money orders from parties you don't know. Particularly if they come from overseas. Much of the phony money orders in circulation today are coming from Africa and Eastern Europe.

HOW TO PREVENT THE SCAM

There are a few commonsense steps you can take to prevent getting scammed by phony money orders:

- Anytime you're doing business with a party you don't personally know and you receive a money order for payment, have the money order verified.[5] Take it to the post office or a bank and have it examined and its serial number validated.

- If you're selling merchandise through eBay, Yahoo! Shopping, or any of the other online shopping bazaars, and the buyer wants to pay you outside the normal business channels (PayPal or credit cards), simply do not accept payment that way. Chances are it's a scam.

- When you receive a money order for an amount greater than the price of any merchandise you are selling, do not refund the difference or cash the money order until you've verified the authenticity of the party you're dealing with and his money order.

- There are ways to help you identify counterfeit postal money orders. Go to http://www.usps.com/postalinspectors.

ALSO SEE: "Shopping Online" (page 188).

---

[5]The same holds true for certified checks. The counterfeit version is hard to spot by the untrained eye.

Cops and Robbers and Outright Thieves

> You can get much farther with a kind word and a gun than you can with a kind word alone.
>
> —AL CAPONE

Some scams are potentially more dangerous to seniors than others. Crimes such as burglaries, robberies, criminals impersonating police officers, and related felonies not infrequently cross the line separating economic harm from physical or emotional harm. Serious stuff indeed, for it is here that seniors are exposed to desperate criminals who don't mind injuring others in the execution of their crimes. Reduce your risk of harm by following the recommendations described in the topics of this section.

Casing Your Home

THE SCAM

You're an elderly couple sitting at home watching TV one afternoon when somebody knocks at your door. You open it[6] and an officious-looking man in a suit flashes a badge. He identifies himself as an examiner with the state social services agency. You let him in and he tells you and your frightened wife that he's been instructed to inspect your home to assure that it meets minimum living standards. You don't know exactly what that means, but you don't want to challenge his authority.

> Never underestimate the shrewdness of a burglar trying to gain access to your home. He'll attempt all manner of disguise to case your home and set it up for burglary.

You offer to accompany the examiner on his inspection tour of your home, but he won't hear of it. He tells you that by law he is

---

[6] A big no-no when you don't know who is on the other side. You should have asked the person to identify himself first by calling through the door. And you should have checked him out through a window or peephole, if possible.

required to make the inspection alone. You accept his word, and you and your wife wait anxiously in the family room of your small house while he conducts his tour. Fifteen minutes later the examiner tells you that you've passed the inspection and leaves. You sigh with relief.

Two days later, while you're at an evening concert, your home is burglarized. The thief steals your wife's jewelry, the cash you had hidden in a closet, and the sterling silver dinner set that's been in your family for two generations. When the police find out about the purported examiner's inspection, they tell you it was the burglar who had cased your home.

HOW TO SPOT THE SCAM

- You have certain fundamental rights as an American citizen that by law cannot be violated:
  - Nobody has the right to examine your home without a properly executed search warrant, so this should have been your first indication that something was wrong.
  - Later, when the so-called examiner told you he was required by law to inspect your home without you being present, that assertion flies in the face of every right you have as an American citizen, and this was your second clue to the scam.
- This scam can take many forms. Besides a government inspector, an employee of the water department might ask to inspect your pipes; a gas company employee might claim you have a dangerous leak in your home and he'll need to check your furnace; somebody who repairs basement walls might say he's spotted a crack on the outside wall and he needs to

inspect the basement and the walls it supports. The list goes on and on. In every instance, you have the right to refuse entry.

HOW TO PREVENT THE SCAM

Here are a few inviolate rules that will help guide your conduct when a so-called person of authority attempts to gain access to your home:

- Deny access to anybody you don't know. Yes, that's difficult to do, and most nice people like yourselves are unaccustomed to refusing anybody with authority, but it's a necessity. Consider it a cardinal rule you must follow to prevent burglaries—or robberies—resulting from imposter scams.[7]
- When somebody on your doorstep claims to be a member of the government, get his name and badge number and ask him to clearly state the agency of the government he works for. If he's up to no good, chances are he'll flee when he knows you're on to him. Should he become truculent, call 911 immediately and ask for the police.
- Ask the person on your doorstep for a telephone number you can call to verify his claim. Then call that telephone number and ask why that government agency wants access to your home. If the claim is a ruse, it will be foiled at this step *before* the crook has a chance to come inside and steal your possessions and harm you.
- If you're frightened about the appearance of the stranger, it

---

[7]Technically, a burglary takes place when the residents aren't home; a robbery when they are. This legal distinction, of course, doesn't mitigate the terror people feel when the safety and security of their homes have been breached.

may be your instincts alerting you. Call 911 without delay and request help.

ALSO SEE: "Fake Meals on Wheels" (page 51); "Police Impersonators" (page 57).

Fake Accidents

THE SCAM

You're driving your new Honda Civic to the supermarket. In the parking lot an old Ford, a clunker, rams into you and damages your fender. You're not hurt, but you are frightened. Nothing like this has ever happened to you before.

The driver of the other car, an angry young man, jumps out and stands at the driver's window of your car, shaking a fist and blaming you for the accident. You know the other driver was at fault, but you cower in your seat because the young man is intimidating. He insists on an immediate payment of $500, which he claims will be necessary to repair the damage done to his car. You're so terrified you write him a check. He leaves and you breathe a sigh of relief. Before you have second thoughts about who was to blame, he's already cashed your check. And come to

> **W**henever you're in your car and feel threatened by a stranger, lock the doors, shut the windows, and lean on the horn until help arrives. If you have a cell phone handy, call 911 and request help.

think of it, didn't you notice in the instant before he crashed into you that his fender was already crumpled?

HOW TO SPOT THE SCAM

Unfortunately there's no way to anticipate this scam because it comes upon you suddenly. But there are steps you can take to protect yourself, as shown below.

HOW TO PREVENT THE SCAM

- If you get into a fender bender and you're not injured, remain in your car and lock the doors. Lower the window an inch or two, just enough to hear the approaching driver when he gets out of his car and walks up to yours.
- If he's belligerent, honk your horn and keep honking it until help arrives. You'll quickly catch somebody's attention. If this is a scam, the other driver may soon flee the scene.
- If the other driver loses his cool and attempts to get you out of the car, step on the gas and drive away, even if your vehicle is damaged, and continue to honk your horn. Crack your window open and scream for help. Drive to a public place like the entrance to a mall and ask somebody to call the police.
- If the other driver isn't hostile but remains intimidating, refuse his demand to be paid on the spot. Tell him you'll be happy to exchange license plate numbers, driver's license numbers, and insurance information with him, but only in the presence of a police officer. Then, if you have a cell phone, dial 911 or ask the other driver to call a police officer. If you don't have a cell phone or the other driver refuses to

make the call, remain in your car and begin honking the horn until you attract the attention of another party. Assuming it's a real accident, the other driver won't have any qualms about requesting a police officer to come to the scene.

- *Remain in your car with the doors locked until a police officer arrives.* If possible, calm yourself enough to get a description of the other driver and his car and its license plate number.

ALSO SEE: "Police Impersonators" (page 57).

Fake Meals on Wheels

THE SCAM

You're an older senior, and you live alone. One mid-morning you answer a knock on the door and a woman in her fifties with gray hair and a pleasant smile tells you she's distributing free meals for seniors. You let her in, not only for the meal, but for a few minutes of talk and companionship.

The woman tells you she needs your Social Security number and Medicaid card so she can charge the meal to Medicaid. You oblige and while you're in another room getting the information from your purse, she rifles through your old rolltop desk. After you return with your Social Security and Medicaid cards, she grabs them and pushes you down on the sofa and removes the twenty dollars you have in your purse. She then leaves. She isn't from Meals on Wheels.

> **M**eals on Wheels and other senior service organizations don't solicit door-to-door. If somebody knocks on your door and claims otherwise, stay inside, lock your doors, and dial 911.

HOW TO SPOT THE SCAM

The example cited above happened recently in Atlanta. A woman stole cash and personal information from several elderly seniors before she was caught. The police issued a bulletin to senior communities alerting seniors to the fraud. They stated the best way to spot this scam is that Meals on Wheels and other organizations that provide meals for seniors do not solicit door-to-door.

HOW TO PREVENT THE SCAM

This is a terrible scam that preys on the oldest seniors, those who are disabled or incapacitated. Those unfortunate souls should follow these rules:

- Fight your urge for companionship when somebody you don't know knocks on your door and offers you something for nothing. Chances are it's a scam.
- Don't be fooled if the scammer is some kindly looking older gent or lady. Thieves come in both genders and all ages. And most of them appear as friendly as sweet Aunt Bea on the old *Andy Griffith Show*—until you open the door.
- Meals on Wheels and other senior services do not usually go door-to-door. Become automatically suspicious of anybody claiming to do so.

ALSO SEE: "Casing Your Home"(page 44).

Con Games

THE SCAM

A con game is a swindle based on a crook's ability to win the confidence and even the sympathy of his mark. Seventy percent of all con games are directed against seniors because of their vulnerability and the perception of their wealth.[8]

There are so many con games floating around that it's impossible to list all of them. The following are representative examples of miscellaneous swindles that occur frequently:

The phony package delivery, the hundred-dollar Bible, the fortune-teller con, three-card monte, and poker night with the boys are examples of scams plied by confidence men and women.

- Phony package delivery: You're sitting in your living room when the doorbell rings. It's a man dressed in the familiar brown UPS uniform holding a package in his hands. He says

[8]According to the Texas Department of Protective and Regulatory Services (http://www.greaterdallascrimecomm.org/elderly_fraud.htm), referring to the entire country.

it's a COD.[9] for your neighbor who isn't home. It costs $33.50, and he was wondering if you might sign for it and pay the charge. He hastens to assure you that your neighbor will pay for delivery, and if you don't pay for it now, your neighbor will have to wait in a long line at the UPS office to get it. You pay and accept the package. When your neighbor arrives home from work at the end of the day, you hand him the package and he opens it to find a large rock. You (or your neighbor, if you're lucky enough to talk him into paying the charge—but don't count on it) are out $33.50.

- The hundred-dollar Bible: In this offensive swindle, scammers read the obituary columns in newspapers, find the addresses of widows and widowers, then call on them, claiming that the deceased ordered a special Bible for the spouse before he or she died, and it's now ready for delivery. Count on paying a hundred dollars or so for a Bible the scammer probably stole from a hotel room.

- The fortune-teller con: If you're a senior who enjoys having your fortune read by fortune-tellers, you are a prime target for a slick scam. Some of these purported fortune-tellers are so engaging they can uncover how much money you're worth and where you keep it. Then they go to work, prophesizing a dark cloud in your future (death, disability, loss of fortune, and so forth), but don't despair, they may be able to prevent the unhappy event by helping you make the right life decisions. They insidiously worm their way into your confidence and sucker you into frequent returns at exorbitant fees for their "services." The greedier ones will sell your personal information to identity thieves.

[9]Cash on delivery.

- Three-card monte: Perhaps you're one of those people who love to gamble and you can't resist making bets. You visit a flea market one Sunday afternoon, and one of these slick sleight-of-hand card sharks suckers you into a game of three-card monte, where for a bet of twenty bucks you have to guess where just one of the cards winds up after the shark has shuffled them around. No matter how closely you watch his hands, you lose every time. You'll never outguess the card shark.

- Poker night with the boys: Often card sharks will talk seniors into a "friendly" game of poker. The con artist flashes a large roll of bills to show he has the cash to play. If you're that senior, you're simply out of your league if you believe you can beat the grifter at his own game. You're not going to do it, and you probably will lose a bundle in the process. If you lose and don't have the cash to pay, he'll take your credit card number. You know what to expect then, don't you?

HOW TO SPOT THE SCAM

Anytime a stranger approaches you, or you're attracted to something a stranger is doing, and there's money involved (your money of course), the warning flags should go up. It doesn't matter what the con game is; if you decide to play, you'll be the loser and the con artist will walk away, chuckling, with your money in his pocket.

HOW TO PREVENT THE SCAM

There are a few rules that will protect you from scams such as those just described:[10]

---

[10]These suggestions are based on recommendations found on the Web site http://www.crimes-of-persuasion.com.

- Never hand over money or give your credit card number to a stranger, no matter how persuasive he may be.
- Don't gamble with anyone you've just met. It could mean good-bye to your cash, your car, or your home.
- Don't be fooled by anybody flashing a large wad of bills; you're not going to get your hands on it.
- Be wary of fortune-tellers. Many are scam artists.
- Accept only pre-paid packages for a neighbor unless you make other arrangements.
- Never accept anything like a Bible from a delivery business that you didn't personally order. You're most vulnerable for this scam at a time of great stress, like after the death of a loved one.

ALSO SEE: "*The Pigeon Drop Scam*" *(page 62);* "*Weight-Loss Pills and Diet Scams*" *(page 90).*

Police Impersonators

THE SCAM

You're a seventy-eight-year-old man driving along a major highway one afternoon, when an unmarked sedan pulls alongside you and the driver rolls down his window and yells "Police. Get off at the next exit." He signals you off the highway onto an access road.

You're scared to death. You grew up in a generation that respected authority and always tried to stay on the right side of the law. *What does he want with me?*

The police officer pulls in behind you as

> When somebody claiming to be a police officer asks for money, don't hand it over. Ask to see his badge and ID and ask for a phone number you can call to verify that he's truly a police officer. That will chase an imposter away.

you park. He climbs out of his car, walks up to you, and identifies himself as a detective lieutenant from the county sheriff's office. He asks to see your driver's license and car registration. You comply with trembling hands. He informs you that you were exceeding the speed limit; if you go to court the fine will be $800. You don't think you were going that fast, but the officer's sudden appearance has left your heart pounding. He tells you the court docket is full and the court would be willing to settle for less if you pay $500 now and avoid court time. You hastily agree and write a check to cash (at the officer's direction). Before you have a chance to settle down and come to your senses, this scammer will have cashed your check.

HOW TO SPOT THE SCAM

A phony police officer may try to persuade you to pay a fine on the spot. Tell him you would rather mail in your fine or appear in court and pay your fine then. You have every right to appear before a magistrate to plead your case, so don't let him tell you otherwise.

HOW TO PREVENT THE SCAM

- If a police officer stops you, particularly one dressed in plain clothes and driving an unmarked car,[11] immediately ask to see his badge and photo identification. If he doesn't have any, drive away. Just to be on the safe side, lock your doors before he approaches until you've seen his identification and you're positive he's an officer. Keep your engine idling.
- *Never* hand out cash on the spot to somebody claiming to be a police officer.
- Do not hand over your driver's license and registration until you're sure he is who he says he is. If you're unsure, call 911 for help.

---

[11]A car not clearly marked "police" or the appropriate law agency identification in bold letters on both sides (such as "Sheriff's Department").

- If you don't carry a cell phone, keep your doors locked and lean on the horn until help arrives.
- If he becomes threatening or abusive, drive away and keep on the horn until you arrive at a safe, populated location, like the parking lot of a Wal-Mart.
- Report the incident immediately to the nearest police station.

ALSO SEE: "Casing Your Home" (page 44); "Fake Accidents" (page 48); "The Pigeon Drop Scam" (page 62).

Slave Reparations

THE SCAM

You're an elderly African-American couple living on Social Security and a relatively small pension the husband earned after thirty years working for the U.S. Postal Service. Money is tight but you're getting by. One day you receive an official-looking envelope in the mail and you open the letter. It's a notice from the govern-

> **S**lave reparations have not been approved by any governing body in the USA. When somebody claims he or she can get you reparations, it's a scam. Report that person to the police.

ment informing you that Congress has passed a slave reparations act. All African-Americans over the age of sixty are eligible to receive a lump-sum payment. You're instructed to submit your Social Security numbers in the self-addressed stamped envelope for purposes of identification, along with your bank account number so you can receive a direct deposit of $10,000 to your account, which is your share of the reparations.

You do so, and ten days later your bank account has been

cleaned out, and thieves have used your Social Security numbers to get credit cards and open charge accounts at large retailers, where they have made large purchases. Needless to say, you receive no reparations. You've been stung.

HOW TO SPOT THE SCAM

There is no slave reparations act. You could have quickly uncovered the scam by calling the Social Security office or any other government office, for that matter, not to mention the local office of the NAACP. If such a bill had been passed by Congress and signed into law by the president, you would have read about it in newspapers and magazines and heard about it on radio and TV.

HOW TO PREVENT THE SCAM

Anytime you receive a letter, telephone call, or e-mail describing slave reparations, contact your local Social Security office immediately, or call the Office of the Inspector General, toll-free at 1-800-269-0471. If you've mistakenly sent the information requested, be sure to mention that.

The Pigeon Drop Scam

THE SCAM

You're taking the afternoon air one lovely day in the spring. As you pass an alleyway, you notice a leather attaché case sticking out from under the corner of a Dumpster and a man reaching underneath attempting to extract it, but having difficulty. You and another man approach the Dumpster at the same time and offer help.

> **F**inding a lot of money is a dream, not a reality. It's rarer than winning the grand lottery. If you come across such money, it's a scam. You're about to lose a pile of your own money.

The three of you manage to pull out the attaché and open it. You see what appear to be financial certificates of some sort. One of the men whistles and says that the financial certificates are bearer bonds worth $25,000. The other man suggests that you turn the bonds in to the police. The first man says that anybody can cash bearer bonds legitimately, and you and he nix the idea. Not exactly the ethical thing to do, but what the heck.

The three of you agree to split the money equally once a

banker has inspected the bonds to assure they're not counterfeit. You tell the other two men you'll take the bonds to your bank for the inspection. The other two aren't exactly doubting you, but they're unsure of your trustworthiness because none of you know one another, and you'll be holding the bonds. One of the men suggests that you put up $3,000 as good-faith money, which will be refunded when the bonds are cashed. You agree. You write them a check for three grand and you never see the men again. The bonds, indeed, are counterfeit.

HOW TO SPOT THE SCAM

What happened to you is what the police call a pigeon drop scam, and you're the pigeon. If you can get past the exhilaration of unexpectedly finding money, you'll reason that bonds or any other valuables worth thousands of dollars are rarely found on the street under Dumpsters or anywhere else. Sure, miracles do happen, but only in novels and movies.

HOW TO PREVENT THE SCAM

- Pigeon drop scammers count on greed interfering with your normally good judgment. You never know when you're going to stumble across twenty-five grand, but in my opinion this is less likely to happen than winning a million-dollar lottery.[12] You should have immediately become suspicious.
- As a general rule, anytime you encounter a situation that's beyond the routine of your life and experience, such as finding a large amount of money, step back, take a deep

[12]No, I'm not a statistician, but you get the point, don't you?

breath, and ask yourself if what you're seeing is real. Examine the people involved and the circumstances. A moment of introspection may prevent you from being scammed.

- What you should have done in the example above is refuse to pay to hold the bonds; instead walk to the nearest bank with the other two men and have a banker authenticate the bonds. Of course, the other two men will depart before then because you're about to uncover their scam.

ALSO SEE: "*Con Games*" *(page 53);* "*Police Impersonators*" *(page 57).*

Health and Medicine

A big lie is more plausible than the truth.

—ERNEST HEMINGWAY

This category, probably more than others in this book, is especially relevant for seniors. They are in the twilight of their years and are more susceptible to health problems than other age groups. And, of course, scammers congregate here like vultures to pick the bones clean. Well, let's not give them the opportunity. Read the following topics carefully and learn how to avoid health and medicine scams.

Health Clubs

THE SCAM

Although you just turned sixty-five, you're in excellent physical shape and intend to stay that way. Unfortunately, you are no longer able to play tennis and volleyball because your knees are giving out, and the last thing you want is to endure the misery of knee replacements. So you decide to try a health club—a gym where you can lift weights to pre-serve your muscular strength and run on a treadmill and climb stairs on a StairMaster to maintain cardiovascular fitness.

> Unless you live in a rural area where the choice is limited, you shouldn't have any trouble finding a health club or gym that doesn't charge start-up fees or require annual contracts. Check with your doctor before starting.

You visit one of the large national health clubs, and the minute you set foot in the door, you're besieged by a saleslady. She tries to sell you a membership to the club. You listen attentively because you're nothing if not unfailingly polite. After she finishes her spiel, you ask the costs. You're astounded to learn there is a $150 up-front fee and the annual dues are $480. The club's personal trainers charge $80 an hour should you elect to have them train you, and the saleslady pushes you to use them. You're also required to sign an annual contract.

If you agree, you're being taken to the cleaners; there's a better way to go.

HOW TO SPOT THE SCAM

Commissioned salespeople at health clubs realize that the influx of new members is greatest in January when people resolve to get back in shape for the new year. They also know that most members drop out after three months. So they push hard to sell as many memberships as they can at that time, knowing that business will stall out about March, along with their commissions. Their job is the archetype of high-pressure salesmanship; when they're applying the pressure to join, you'll feel as if your head is being squeezed in a vise.

You have options. There are many health clubs and gyms out there that are not so rapacious as the one described above. The gym I belong to, for example, charges seniors $30 a month for unlimited use. You can go month-to-month without purchasing a contract. There is no initiation fee and the personal trainers charge $50 per hour, if you decide to use them (but you don't have to, and they don't pressure you). The gym is quite large and contains many machines, free weights, benches, and separate rooms for classes.

HOW TO PREVENT THE SCAM

Working out is important for seniors. It prevents muscles from atrophying, reduces stress, and is great for the heart. But it can be a costly experience. To prevent being scammed:

- Opt for a health club that has monthly fees, one where no contract is required. Some health insurance companies, such as Blue Cross of Georgia, will even pay for the health club; you work out at no charge.
- Get your doctor's approval before you start.
- Don't be pressured into using expensive personal trainers if you can't see the need for them. But if you don't, read a weight-training manual, like the one *Muscle & Fitness* publishes, that shows you how to avoid injuring yourself. Your library should have several such manuals, or you can buy one at a bookstore.

Laser Eye Clinics

THE SCAM

Here's a little-known insight: some ophthalmologists who operate laser eye clinics like to operate with lasers—whether they're needed or not. Why? Because there's more money in it than routine eye exams. Seniors are targets for this scam because many of them are less likely to question the advice of medical professionals.

Find it too incredible to be true? Well, it happened to me.

I'm a seventy-one-year-old diabetic who takes an annual dilated eye exam to detect

> **D**octors get greedy, too. Sometimes they prescribe treatments that are unnecessary, to collect from that great cash cow, Medicare. It behooves you to get a second opinion for any major diagnosis.

retinopathy because diabetics are especially susceptible to developing eye disease. I had the same ophthalmologist for fifteen years until my insurance company no longer covered his practice.[13] I didn't have any luck with my next ophthalmologist either because the insurance company cancelled him after two years.

Neither of the two ophthalmologists I used for those seventeen years found any developing eye disease after examining me. Thankfully, I was consistently given a clean bill of health.

I wasn't as lucky with my next ophthalmologist. He ran a laser eye clinic as part of his practice, and told me after a dilated eye exam that I would soon need laser surgery. He scheduled me for a return dilated eye exam in three months, with surgery to probably follow immediately after.

Of course, that scared the living daylights out of me. The first word that runs through a diabetic's mind when he flunks an eye exam is "blindness," a frequent end result for diabetics who have failed to maintain good glucose control over the years.

But I *had* maintained good control, and I was suspicious. I returned to my original ophthalmologist and paid the bill out of my own pocket for a dilated eye exam. I was relieved to find that my eyes were in good shape. To make doubly sure, I visited yet another ophthalmologist and found the same pleasing result.

The inevitable conclusion was that the laser eye clinic ophthalmologist was selling instead of prescribing, and lining his pockets at my expense. Pretty reprehensible, isn't it?

HOW TO SPOT THE SCAM

So, what's the best way to detect this scam? Use your common sense. If nothing was wrong with your eyes before, and the oph-

---

[13]The sad fact is that spiraling medical costs are causing more and more insurance companies to stop covering some doctors' practices. And more and more doctors are opting out from health plans because of shrinking coverage combined with high paperwork requirements.

thalmologist unexpectedly discovers a problem, that's a red flag. The same holds true for any medical condition you have. As the Italian proverb says, "To trust is good. Not to trust is better."

HOW TO PREVENT THE SCAM

Unfortunately, you can't always rely on what medical profession-als tell you. In the final analysis, you are responsible for selecting the right course of action. Here's what to do:

- If you find yourself in a situation similar to mine for any health problem, not just your eyes, get a second opinion. And a third if necessary. Don't accept a negative diagnosis if your instincts and common sense tell you otherwise. Damn shame it's necessary, but don't close your eyes to the fact that some doctors get greedy.
- Report the scoundrel to the American Medical Association and Better Business Bureau. And don't forget to file a complaint with your state's consumer affairs office or attorney general.
- You might also complain to your insurance company. They have experts on staff who investigate insurance fraud.[14]

[14]Speaking of eye surgery, NBC Channel Four in Washington, DC, exposed a bait-and-switch tactic used by a laser eye clinic. It seems the clinic advertised corrective eye surgery for $299 an eye. Several patients complained they were charged up to $799 an eye but told only *after* the surgery was completed. "The Real Deal: Lasik," broadcast Oct. 31, 2003, by consumer reporter Liz Crenshaw.

Living Wills

THE SCAM

The Terri Schiavo case in Florida has undoubtedly made you aware of the necessity of prescribing your manner of death should you lapse into a helpless vegetative state. After reading an advertisement in a local shopping newsletter, you send away for a living will form for $19.95. What you're unaware of is that these forms are available free as downloads from the Internet, as well as from local sources such as your hospital or legal aid society.

Worse, you answer an ad in the paper advertising free living wills, and before you've had a chance to take a deep breath, a slick salesman shows up on your doorstep trying to peddle dubious investment products.

A living will is a document all seniors need if they want to control the manner of their death. Get your form at no cost from your local legal aid society or hospital, or download one free online.

HOW TO SPOT THE SCAM

Any company spending money to advertise living wills is after something; that something is your money. Don't fall for this scam. Avoid the unpleasant necessity of listening to the high-pressure blather of a scam artist trying to sell you investment products or services you don't want and don't need.

HOW TO PREVENT THE SCAM

Get your free living will form or durable power of attorney for health care form from your local legal society. If you're uncomfortable with the legalities of the form, have an attorney complete it for you. The cost should be relatively cheap.

Note: The difference between a living will and durable power of attorney for health care is that the latter appoints an agent to oversee execution of the living will. The stand-alone living will appoints no such agent and is merely your intention regarding end-of-life care.

ALSO SEE: "Investment Schemes" (page 125).

Medical Breakthroughs

THE SCAM

Like many seniors, your name is on mailing lists for people interested in new medical products and tips for healthy living. You receive a call one afternoon from a nice-sounding lady asking if you've heard of the latest medical product breakthrough for seniors suffering from high blood pressure, a product she describes as revolutionary. Since you're combating high blood pressure, you're eager to hear more and she arranges for a "health technologist" to visit you a few days hence.

You have the obligation to stay current with medical developments for afflictions you have. If you do, you won't be fooled into shelling out money to scammers for phony cures.

The so-called health technologist arrives, and she is really a high-pressure saleswoman. In glowing terms, she describes a new vitamin compound she claims will reduce your systolic and diastolic blood pressure by a dozen points each. After her sales pitch, she pushes you to buy a three-month supply of the vitamin compound for $450. She talks you into buying it because, as she says, "This is an introductory price and today is its last day at this price." You buy and are dismayed to find that after a month's use it hasn't reduced either your systolic or diastolic blood pressure one iota. You've been scammed.

HOW TO SPOT THE SCAM

There were two clues. The telephone call was the first. Real medical breakthroughs are seldom introduced to the public this way. They almost always arrive via your health practitioner's office or hospital. So you should automatically be suspicious. The second clue trails the first: the arrival of a so-called health technologist on your doorstep, the sure sign of an impending high-pressure sales pitch.

HOW TO PREVENT THE SCAM

Anytime you receive a call or letter describing a breakthrough medical product, take the following steps *before* you buy in:

- First, verify the reality of the "medical breakthrough" by contacting your primary physician or medical specialist, in this case a cardiologist. A simple call to your cardiologist would have quickly exposed the scam.
- Second, if medical equipment is involved, and it looks as if the equipment might actually help you, check to see if renting or leasing it would be cheaper than buying it.

- Next, be sure that Medicare or your supplemental insurance carrier covers the cost.
- Finally, if a contract for renting or purchasing the equipment is involved, ask a lawyer to review it before you commit.

ALSO SEE: "Door-to-Door Salesmen" (page 176).

Medicare Prescription Drug Plans

THE SCAM

A salesman calls you with an offer to sell a Medicare-approved prescription drug plan that offers a 15 percent discount over and above the cheapest plan on the market. He says he's practically giving the plan away for fifty bucks. You think this is a pretty good deal because Medicare-approved prescription drug plans all carry a monthly premium.

> Medicare prescription drug plans are offered by private companies authorized by Medicare, and nobody else. Ignore solicitations from companies that offer discounts, for these discounts do not exist.

The extra 15 percent will sure come in handy. You pay three months up front, only to find the first time you try to use it that it's phony. You lost fifty bucks. And you're still not enrolled in a prescription drug plan.

HOW TO SPOT THE SCAM

It's a violation of federal law to solicit Medicare prescription drug plans (or any other Medicare product or service) door-to-door or by telephone.[15] Therefore, anybody selling Medicare prescription drug plans door-to-door or by telephone is a fraud and should be immediately reported to the police.

HOW TO PREVENT THE SCAM

Knowledge, as they say, is power. You'll be able to reduce your vulnerability to scams of this nature by following these guidelines:

- Go to the Web site http:/www.medicare.gov and find out what companies are approved to sell Medicare prescription drug plans for your state. The Web site also lists specific drugs covered by each plan[16] and locations of pharmacies by zip code.
- If you suspect a fraud, call 1-800-MEDICARE the Fraud Hotline of the Health and Human Services Office of the Inspector General at 1-800-447-8477.
- *Consumer Reports* has a Web site devoted to advising you on the cheapest and safest drugs available, including a list of generic drugs. You can find it online at http://www.CRBest-BuyDrugs.org.

---

[15]The government allows private health insurance carriers to provide information door-to-door or by mail, but draws the line at allowing them to ask consumers to enroll.

[16]Called the "formulary" by Medicare.

- May I also suggest that you compare prices at discount chains such as Costco and Target? They may be cheaper than going the Medicare prescription drug plan route, depending on what drugs you need and how often you take them.[17] Also, drugs purchased through reputable Canadian pharmacies frequently have offered lower prices for the same drugs sold in the USA. This option may not last if both American and Canadian governments decide to stop Americans from buying drugs outside the country. Stay tuned.

ALSO SEE: "Online Pharmacies" (page 86); "Medicare Fraud" (page 80).

---

[17]If you qualify for the low-income provision of a Medicare-approved prescription drug plan, this might be the cheapest route for you to go. Check to see if you qualify online at http://www.medicare.gov. Also some Costco and Target pharmacies participate in the Medicare plan.

Medicare Fraud

THE SCAM

As a senior you're subject to any number of schemes that clever scammers devise to defraud Medicare, using you as an unknowing accomplice. These include[18]

- Rolling lab schemes: You're shopping at your local mall when you spot a booth where (what appear to be) nurses in white uniforms are checking blood levels of shoppers for cholesterol, fats, and triglycerides. At no cost. Your primary physician didn't order the tests, but you decide to take them anyway. Hey, it's free! Unknown to you, this lab moves from mall to mall as well as retirement home to retirement home,

Medicare fraud is one of the most pervasive and expensive frauds in the USA. Prevent the scammers from using your name to bilk the government by getting approval for all medical procedures from your doctor.

[18]Based on information contained on the Medicare Web site. Go to: http://www.medicare.gov/fraudabuse/tips.asp.

bilking Medicare for unwanted and unnecessary tests not ordered by doctors. This rolling lab stays one step ahead of the sheriff. If Medicare discovers the scam, it may bill you for the tests, which amount to several hundred dollars.

- Medical equipment schemes: You've got a pronounced limp but it hasn't hindered your everyday activities. A saleswoman talks you into receiving a free motorized walker. You don't really need it, but it's handy to have. Medicare is billed ten grand. When Medicare finds out, you're in a heap of trouble.
- Services not performed: Your nephew Rolf, who runs a pharmacy, submits false claims to Medicare on your behalf. You know about it, but say nothing, thereby giving Rolf tacit approval. He's been cheating for years and getting away with it. Total cost to Medicare: $170,000 . . . so far. Could be jail time for Rolf if he's found out, and, you may be tagged as his accomplice.

In all of the scams mentioned above, Medicare thieves either forge a doctor's signature or get a crooked doctor to sign his or her name for a cut of the illegal proceeds.

HOW TO SPOT THE SCAM

Always check with your physician before taking any tests or ordering any medical equipment or supplies. She's a professional in the best position to detect scams.

I can almost hear you asking: "Well, suppose she's scamming Medicare herself? How will I know?" You probably won't know, but if you follow the steps outlined on page 82, you should avoid most problems of this sort. You *don't* want your good name associated with Medicare fraud.

HOW TO PREVENT THE SCAM

The FBI recommends that seniors follow these guidelines:

- Don't sign blank insurance forms or give carte blanche authority to a medical provider to do so for you.
- Conduct no medical business outside of the authority of your primary physician. If your insurance doesn't require a primary physician, then ask your insurance company for approval before making any purchase of medical products or services.
- Keep records and receipts of drugs purchased, tests taken, and examinations conducted. A paper trail may help you if you're suspected of trying to bypass Medicare regulations.
- Hand out your Medicare and supplemental health insurance cards *only* to medical providers you know and who are on approved Medicare and supplemental health insurance lists.
- Never do business with anybody who is offering to give you something for free without first checking with Medicare or your supplemental health insurance company.

ALSO SEE: "Medicare Prescription Drug Plans" (page 77).

Nursing Homes

THE SCAM

The list of abuses at nursing homes across the USA is staggering. Those abuses include fraud, neglect, sexual abuse, rampant drug use, violence, improper medication, malpractice, theft, nursing oversights, and nursing homes staffed by criminals. For an eye-opening revelation go online to Consumer Affairs (http://www.consumeraffairs.com/news_index/nursing_home.html) and read nursing home stories from across the country that will make your blood curdle.

If your mother or father is in need of a nursing home, I would seriously consider an alternative, if possible. If not, be aware that although there are 17,000 nursing homes across the country, and while I'm sure most of them are legitimate and meet federal and state guidelines, many do not. It could

> Think twice before sending a parent or grandparent to a nursing home. The industry is plagued with problems that might shock you into changing your mind unless you're careful in making the right choice.

be just your bad luck that Mom or Dad winds up in an institution where abuse is rampant.

HOW TO SPOT THE SCAM

The federal Nursing Home Reform Act specifies that a nursing home ". . . must provide services and activities to attain or main-tain the highest practicable physical, mental, and psycho-social well-being of each resident in accordance with a written plan of care . . ."

Unfortunately, as you will discover in your research, this doesn't always happen. And abuse and malpractice aren't always immediately apparent. You need to dig beneath the surface to uncover the horror stories.

HOW TO PREVENT THE SCAM

- First, go online to the Medicare Web site, http://www. medicare.gov, and find the Nursing Home Compare link (type "nursing home" in the search box at the top of the page). This opens a page where you can look up nursing homes by state, county, zip code, or by the nursing home's name. Nursing Home Compare describes such information as staffing, quality of care, ratings on deficiencies and patient mistreatment, and reported problems such as the nursing home's history of complaints for abuse and neglect. It even shows staff hours worked per resident per day, and the number of residents in physical restraints. This Web site is a good starting point.
- Next, make sure you visit the nursing home. Walk around and get a good feel for the place: Is it sanitary? Does the staff

look as if it's interested in the patients? Do patient-residents seem content? Does it smell clean? There's much you can discover by a walk-through.

- Get references. Ask the opinions of others who have parents in the nursing home. And check into the possibility of assisted living. Most such facilities are owned and run by private companies and the cost varies. But it provides a viable option to nursing homes.

- Finally, do your online research. Write in the nursing home's name in a search engine like Google and see what it reveals. If there are complaints registered against the home, chances are you'll find them online.

Online Pharmacies

THE SCAM

Like most seniors, your insurance doesn't cover all of your prescription drug costs, even with Medicare's help. With the price of Medicare's drugs escalating every year, you need to either obtain financial assistance or buy drugs at reduced prices, a common problem among seniors.

You can buy drugs online at discounts. The danger is that many online pharmacies disappear overnight, and some sell adulterated or under-strength drugs. Deal only with certified suppliers.

You turn to online pharmacies, a recent phenomenon that has blossomed into a large-scale business providing accessibility to common drugs, many at heavily discounted prices. You apply to one such online pharmacy and find that ordering drugs online is a lot faster and easier than through pharmacies in your neighborhood. Your first month's order comes to $185, substantially lower than the $310 you usually shell out every month. You're ecstatic.

The bubble bursts a month later when, the drugs not yet hav-

ing arrived by mail, you go online to find the pharmacy you ordered from no longer exists. The authorities tell you it was a scam
that never delivered its first batch of drugs.

HOW TO SPOT THE SCAM

The Internet is chock full of online pharmacies, many of them
legitimate, some of them not. The legitimate ones such as http://
www.drugstore.com or http://www.walgreens.com operate like
traditional "brick-and-mortar" pharmacies in your town. They are
licensed by the state medical boards they operate in, and they
validate prescriptions from doctors before dispensing drugs.

Here's one of the clues to a legitimate online pharmacy: its
insistence on requiring you to either mail or fax in a prescription
from your doctor. The more suspect online pharmacies may not
demand prescriptions and may substitute online medical consultations from them for a fee before shipping a medication. Pharmacies like these are often located outside the United States in
countries such as Nigeria. Buyer beware!

HOW TO PREVENT THE SCAM

If your doctor recommends an online pharmacy (and many of
them do, especially Canadian pharmacies they're familiar with),
chances are that drugs from that particular pharmacy are both
safe and cheap.

- You will have few problems with sites such as http://www.
  drugstore.com and http://www.CVS.com, which have been
  certified by the National Association of Boards of Pharmacy
  (NABP) as Verified Internet Pharmacy Practice Sites

(VIPPS). To be VIPPS-certified, a pharmacy must comply with the licensing and inspection requirements of each state in which it dispenses pharmaceuticals, offer secure records transfer, and provide meaningful consultations between patients and pharmacists. So look for the VIPPS certification displayed on the Web site of the online pharmacy you choose. You can verify a pharmacy's VIPPS certification by visiting the Web site of the National Association of Boards of Pharmacy at http://www.nabp.net/vipps/intro.asp.

- More and more online pharmacies are being certified by Health Internet Ethics (Hi-Ethics), a coalition of Internet health sites. Hi-Ethics focuses on content labeling, as opposed to VIPPS, which focuses on drug dispensation. Look for this certification as a further measure of legitimacy.

- If you're interested in purchasing heavily discounted drugs overseas, go online to http://www.overseaspharmacy.com. The owner of the Web site vouches for reputable online pharmacies from places as far away as Asia and New Zealand (although you should be aware that the risks are higher for receiving adulterated or low-potency drugs from some overseas sources). Once you have identified a pharmacy you want to do business with, I strongly suggest that you contact some of their customers to substantiate their legitimacy. And of more importance, *don't forget to get your doctor's opinion.* Keep in mind that the FDA forbids the importation of drugs.

- Finally, remember these three points:
  - Not all online pharmacies sell drugs that are cheaper than brick-and-mortar pharmacies. It pays to shop and compare.
  - Most online prescriptions handled by Canadian pharmacies and many overseas pharmacies truly do have lower prices.

- Some online pharmacies have yet to develop systems needed to handle your co-pay with health insurance companies. This is a particularly troubling point with overseas pharmacies. To avoid throwing away scare dollars, check with your insurance company first.

ALSO SEE: "Medicare Prescription Drug Plans" (page 77).

Weight-Loss Pills and Diet Scams

THE SCAM

You're a newly retired couple, both in your late fifties. Life has been pretty good to you, but you would like to lose some pounds and remain healthy. Over the years you've tried every diet imaginable, from Dr. Atkins to the grapefruit regimen. Sure, the weight comes off for a while during the spring and summer, but always seems to creep back over the winter months.

> There is no magic pill to wash away the pounds. Nor is there a magic diet that will do the trick. Consult a doctor or nutritionist before embarking on a diet that could lighten your wallet and even harm you.

At the senior center where you exercise, one of your friends tells you about an amazing new weight-loss diet that really and truly works. She swears by it. The essence of the program is a pill that liquefies your fat cells, which are then washed away in body waste. The great part about it is that you can eat anything you want. You get the name of the program and its telephone number and make the call. A persuasive salesman talks you into trying the program for ninety days; he guarantees weight loss *if you follow the program's instructions.* You pay $140 for both you and your wife.

You follow the program's instructions religiously. After ninety days, not only have you not lost weight, both you and your wife have put on a few extra pounds. You call the salesman and (you guessed it) he claims you couldn't have followed the program to the letter. You've been scammed to the tune of $140.

HOW TO SPOT THE SCAM

If the weight-loss pill or diet program makes claims or statements like those shown below, it's probably a fake:

- Pills that melt away the pounds.
- An ab belt that reduces your waist size.
- Weight-loss without exercise or dieting.
- Eat anything you want and as much as you want and still lose weight.
- Testimonials from so-called doctors (more likely, actors dressed in white lab coats) and institutions you and the American Medical Association have never heard of.
- Case histories that sound too good to be true. ("Golly, I ate a quart of ice cream every night and still lost twenty-five pounds in three months.")
- This amazing diet supplement is available from this company *only* and no others.
- Words in the ad such as "miraculous weight loss you won't believe," "ancient Chinese formula," and "secret ingredients."

HOW TO PREVENT THE SCAM

Anytime you hear about or receive promotional material on the latest, greatest advance in weight-loss technology:

- Ask the opinion of your doctor or another medical professional you trust.
- Call the dietician or nutritionist at your local hospital and ask her to comment on the weight-loss program. These are the kind of people who will be most aware of any advances in weight loss and diet, and in a position to make recommendations.
- Get references of people who lost weight. Talk to them, but be careful they're not paid shills for the company selling the weight-loss program. You can often tell the difference: paid actors recite lines that sound like lines in a play. People like you and I will come across as genuine.

ALSO SEE: "Con Games" (page 53).

Insurance

Insurance is what most people call a necessary evil. It's costly and provides no immediate benefits, but we all know if we get sick and don't have any insurance it can bankrupt us. Or if we get in a car accident and don't have any coverage, the resulting lawsuits could drain our savings. Or if our house burns down and we had let the insurance premiums lapse, we could be out on the street, homeless.

Still, there are some kinds of coverage that aren't needed; they're an unnecessary expense. There are also some insurance policies around that don't pay off when they're supposed to. This section describes both situations and shows you how to deal with them.

Unneeded Insurance Policies

THE SCAM

Insurance is not a scam. All of us at one time or another need insurance to protect against unforeseen events such as health problems, disability, a car accident, or a fire in the home. The scam comes when some slick salesperson talks you into buying an insurance policy you don't need.

Many insurance policies are unneeded and waste your money. If you know which benefit you and which just drain your piggy bank, you can squeeze the most from your insurance dollar.

HOW TO SPOT THE SCAM

Insurance peddlers pressure you to buy a variety of policies that go beyond basic needs such as health insurance, term life insurance, disability insurance, homeowners insurance, and car insurance. Anytime an insurance agent asks you to buy coverage beyond that, question its need. If you follow the guidelines listed below, you should have no problem distinguishing between what is worthwhile and what is unnecessary.

HOW TO PREVENT THE SCAM

Consumer Reports has pulled together a list of insurance policies it says you probably don't need.[19] The following list was adapted from its recommendations:

- Flight insurance: If your flight goes down, your beneficiaries are covered. But how often does that happen? It will cost you up to $60 for a single flight. Why pay when a term life insurance policy (which *Consumer Reports* recommends) covers you anyway? And if you survive the crash, you're covered by your health insurance.
- Identity theft insurance: Good idea but expensive, ranging upwards of $180 annually for $25,000 coverage. But—and this is a big but—it does not include unauthorized charges against your bank account. In its place, protect yourself by following the recommendations in the "Identity Theft" section (page 31).[20] Furthermore, some banks now cover their customers against identity-theft losses at no charge. Yours might be one of those.
- Mortgage life insurance: Pays off the mortgage when you die. But it's very expensive. Rely instead on your term life insurance.
- Car rental insurance: I know about this one from my days traveling. My automobile insurance policy covered me for the

---

[19]*Consumer Reports*, July, 2004, page 49.

[20]Author's recommendation, not *Consumer Reports*.

basics, and my credit card picked up the balance. So why shell out an extra $10 a day to Hertz? No way!

- Cancer insurance: This specialty insurance costs from a few hundred dollars to three grand annually. Use your existing health insurance coverage and save the money.

- Accidental death insurance: Remember the movie *Double Indemnity* where Fred MacMurray and Barbara Stanwyck plot to kill her husband and make it look like an accident so they can collect double the insurance? Well, the cost of movies when you were a kid was about a quarter, and if memory serves, the cost of the policy Fred MacMurray wrote in that movie was about fifty bucks. Today accidental death insurance will set you back six hundred clams a year. Talk about inflation. But why shell out the money when your term life insurance will pay off regardless of how you die?

- Credit card loss insurance: Typical plans cost about $10 to $15 a month. Federal law limits your losses to $50.00. Don't waste your money. Just be more careful about holding on to your credit cards.

- Credit disability insurance: If you become disabled, the policy will pay portions of any outstanding loans up to three years. The cost is about $21 for every thousand dollars of coverage. Instead, a good disability plan, which you should have, will cover those expenses.

- You should also be aware that if you travel overseas and your only insurance is Medicare and you don't have a supplemental insurance policy with a carrier like Blue Cross, you may want to purchase a separate travel insurance policy for the trip. In that case go online to http:// www.naic.org/cis and look up travel insurance carriers. The Web site will alert you to problems consumers have had with travel insurers.

ALSO SEE: "Identity Theft" (page 31); "Fradulent Insurance Companies" (page 98).

Fraudulent Insurance Companies

THE SCAM

Your insurance agent, a woman you have worked with and trusted for almost fifteen years, tells you about a sensational new Medicare supplement policy, one that has reasonable premiums, low co-pays, and offers a drug benefit of $1,000. You enthusiastically agree to switch from you and your wife's current Medicare supplement policies to the new one and, with your insurance agent's help, make out the necessary paperwork and pay an advance premium.

> **M**ost seniors take the legitimacy of insurance policies for granted. Scammers love this because lack of scrutiny hides their frauds. Always check out your new insurer online.

Things go well for the first six months, although other than the drug benefit, you really haven't had any medical problems that would require you to use the policy. Then your wife of fifty-one years gets sick, and unfortunately it's serious. The bills from her surgery and hospital stay climb to over $90,000. That dollar amount, like anything else today having to do with health care, is almost mind numbing. But thankfully you have insurance.

That is, you think you have insurance—until it's time to pay the bills. Your insurance agent calls one day in a panic to tell you that the health insurance company you had faithfully paid premiums to for six months has been run by shady operators who stashed the premiums in overseas accounts and have now skipped the country. You, and many others like you, are without insurance coverage. You don't know what to do or who to turn to. And your insurance agent is distraught because she fell for the scam, too. You're left holding the bag for ninety grand with no one to turn to.

HOW TO SPOT THE SCAM

Here are the red flags that should have alerted you to a scam:

- The deal was too good to be true. No other health insurance company offered as low a co-pay or could match the prescription drug benefit. When a deal is too good to be true, it probably is. This principle holds true for the purchase of any product or service. Don't let the hype blind you to the reality.
- Both you and the agent should have noticed in the insurance company's promotions that it was insuring almost anybody, regardless of past or existing medical conditions, something most legitimate insurers are reluctant to do. You should have asked the question: How can the insurer afford it? The answer is, it couldn't.
- The agent should have noticed that words like "premiums" and "commissions" were missing from the company's promotional material, and in their place were "consultant's

fees" and "contributions." That's a sure sign the health insurer is not a legitimate insurer. Another tip-off: The scam company will avoid the word "insurance" in its promotional literature.

HOW TO PREVENT THE SCAM

- Always, always check out your prospective health care insurer. And don't trust that important safeguard to your insurance agent. She can be fooled, too. Some of these fraudulent companies are so slick that they can, and have, fooled many insurance agents. Go online and type in the name of the insurer in a search engine like Google. If a common thread of complaints surface, consider yourself alerted.
- Here's the real expert: A. M. Best, the recognized authority on rating insurance companies. Use it to check your prospective insurer. Its Web site is packed full of useful information about the insurance industry that will help you avoid making mistakes. Go online to http://www.ambest.com and see what you find.
- Don't bother talking to friends and neighbors who have the same insurance company, unless they've had operations or hospital stays and can attest to the insurer's reliability with paying bills.

ALSO SEE: "Unneeded Insurance Policies" (page 94).

Internet

Never before in history has so much information been available
to so many people. The Internet is both a blessing and a curse.
You can research any topic you desire, buy almost any goods or
services you want online, and connect with people having similar
interests. Unfortunately, you can also make yourself vulnerable
to attack by hackers who want to steal your identity along with
the money in your bank account. But only if you don't follow
some basic rules. Those rules of the information superhighway
are the topics of this section.

Bogus Web Sites

THE SCAM

You've been on the Internet for well over a year now, and you're proud of the facility you've developed, jumping from link[21] to link to find the information you want on a variety of topics. Recently,

you ordered a heavily discounted Apple iPod 60GB MP3 player for $89.99 from a discount warehouse you found by surfing. You never heard of this particular discount warehouse, but it has a very professional Web site, one that took some money to design, so you're reassured about its solidity. You're also quite excited because the top version of Apple's MP3 player you ordered normally sells for $399.00. The way you figure it, you've saved $309.

> Deal with names you're familiar with online. Never hand out your credit card number to a company you haven't heard of. And never answer an e-mail requesting that you supply personal information.

[21]A link is what you click on with your mouse to open other pages of information.

Sorry, you lose. You get a call from your credit card company ten days later claiming you've exceeded your purchase limit of $5,000. You're shocked because during the current credit card billing period your sole use of the credit card was to buy the $89.99 iPod. You rush to go online, only to discover that the discount warehouse's Web site is no longer active. Of course, you never receive the iPod.

You've now joined the ranks of thousands of others who've been scammed on the Internet by a bogus Web site. Welcome to the club.

HOW TO SPOT THE SCAM

Unfortunately, anything you do here is after the fact. You've already given the scammers your credit card number, and imagine what fun they're going to have using it. Often, the scammers gather credit card numbers and sell them to thieves who go on fast spending sprees. Those thieves, frequently in foreign locations, max out the cards as quickly as possible, buying anything and everything from appliances and furniture to furs and jewelry.

HOW TO PREVENT THE SCAM

Principle #1: Never—repeat never—give out your credit card number online to any company you're unfamiliar with. Companies such as Wal-Mart, Sears, Amazon.com, Columbia Records, Barnes & Noble, and Best Buy are familiar names and usually quite safe to order merchandise from online.

I say "usually" because on occasion a hacker with a clever Web design partner may concoct a bogus Web site that impersonates a well-known online retailer or bank.[22] Blatant attempts to cheat you such as this are usually shut down quickly, but buyers who have been cheated will waste no time expressing their outrage online. Check what the blogs and newsgroups have to say by conducting a search of the company. If there are complaints, they're usually going to surface first on the Internet.

Principle #2: Regardless of how well designed and professional-looking a Web site is, the minds behind it may be up to no good. So if you've never heard of the company advertising the product or service, check it out with the Better Business Bureau (BBB) or your state's consumer affairs office to see if it's a bogus company. You might even try an Internet search to see what information you can uncover on the company. Use a search engine like Google or Yahoo! to uncover complaints.

ALSO SEE: "Banking Online" (page 21); "Identity Theft" (page 31); "Dangerous Spam E-mail" (page 105); "Phishing for Your Credit Card Number" (page 110); "Shopping Online" (page 188).

---

[22]See "Banking Online" (page 21) to see how banks are countering this threat.

Dangerous Spam E-mail

THE SCAM

There are untold numbers of ways scam artists prey on seniors through e-mail. They steal their identities, make purchases in upscale stores using their stolen credit card numbers, and empty their bank accounts. The types of fraud perpetrated through careless maintenance of e-mail accounts is a constant threat and growing. Let me repeat: careless maintenance of e-mail accounts. Meaning that most e-mail scams are preventable.

> **D**efeat spam by using disposable e-mail accounts from Web-based services such as Google or Yahoo. When spam overloads your in-box, shut down the account and open another. It's free.

HOW TO SPOT THE SCAM

Spam is defined as unwanted e-mails, usually from parties you don't know, almost always in an attempt to sell you something or uncover personal information such as credit card numbers or

Social Security numbers. If you find yourself receiving an in-
creasing amount of spam e-mail from parties you're not familiar
with, your e-mail address has been compromised and you're in
immediate danger of being scammed.

HOW TO PREVENT THE SCAM

At the first sign of spam, forward the message to whatever service
is providing your e-mail. This will either be your Internet service
provider (ISP) like AOL or ATT Worldnet, or a Web-based e-mail
service like Hotmail or Yahoo.

Most ISPs make it easy to handle spam. When somebody
sends you a spam e-mail, you click on a link that blocks any further spam from that source.

If the amount of spam e-mail continues,[23] the second ave-
nue of defense involves shutting down the e-mail address that
has been compromised. Make sure you actually delete the account. Your ISP or Web-based e-mail service will provide instructions.

Finally, if you follow these simple precautions, your chances
of being successfully attacked by spam will diminish:

- Consider using a Web-based e-mail service such as Yahoo!
  Or Hotmail. They're free and provide a high level of service,
  and as I mentioned above, some offer spam protection.[24] A
  Web-based e-mail address has the further advantage of

[23]Once a spammer gets your e-mail address, he will sell it to other spammers. Before
you realize what's happening, your e-mail address is everywhere.

[24]Some free Web-based e-mail services provide free spam protection while others
don't. You'll need to check.

keeping your same e-mail address if you change ISPs. If you use only your ISP's e-mail service, when you move, for example from AOL to ATT Worldnet, you'll need to change e-mail addresses. That can be a pain in the neck, especially if you have many correspondents.

- Establish two or three Web-based e-mail addresses. If one of the e-mail addresses is accidentally compromised, just delete that account and use one of the others. I, for example, use one Web-based e-mail account for personal e-mail, the other for business. And I do change them if I think my e-mail address has been compromised.

- Virus protection is crucial. Most people surfing the Internet understand this and buy an anti-virus software package (most new computers come with built-in anti-virus programs), but that only covers you for viruses detected as of the date the software was made or updated. Few know that literally dozens of new viruses are discovered daily, which calls for live updates (automatic update protection), a service from your anti-virus software company that costs less than $3 a month and is an absolute requirement. To get automatic update protection, go online to your anti-virus software company and follow instructions for automatic updates. Or, if you prefer to do it on the cheap, get a free online scan for viruses. See appendix B: "Anti-virus Software" (page 239) for online sources.

- Make sure your computer is set to take operating system automatic updates from Microsoft while you're online. It's beyond the purview of this book to show you how. Ask a knowledgeable salesperson at the store where you bought your computer to explain what to do.

- Hackers use spambots[25] to gather e-mail addresses and sell them to spammers. So tell your friends and associates to keep your e-mail address private. That means not inserting it on a copy list sent to dozens of others. People use copy lists when they're broadcasting messages to their friends and associates. It's easier because all they have to do is click the send button once and their message is sent to their entire e-mail list. The more they spread your e-mail address around the Internet, the greater the opportunity for hackers to find it.

- Never open an e-mail attachment from somebody you don't know. Never. Period. And never open an e-mail attachment from some party asking you to validate sensitive information,[26] even though that party claims to be your bank, insurance company, the IRS, police department, Social Security Administration, and so on. Legitimate organizations *never* solicit that kind of information online. It means a hacker is trying to steal your identity.

- I would also recommend going a step further and not opening an e-mail (not just an attachment—the e-mail itself) from people or organizations you don't know or from parties you're not expecting to hear from. This might sound a trifle extreme, but it sure will keep you from lowering your guard and opening up your computer to hackers.

- If you have a Web site and want to post your e-mail address there so other people can contact you, write your e-mail address this way: "Johnjones at hotmail.com" (replace "at"

---

[25]Software designed to roam the Internet and "harvest" e-mail addresses.

[26]Credit card number, bank account number, Social Security number, date of birth, mother's maiden name. You get the picture.

with "@"). This will prevent the spambots from harvesting your e-mail address because they can't interpret the word "at."[27]

- Consider surfing the Internet using an anonymous surfer. This is software that allows you to visit any page you desire on the Internet without leaving an identification trail. In other words, the fact that you visited a Web site will not be recorded. By extension, this means you can send anonymous e-mail without the receiving party knowing where it came from. When you avoid a trail, you're adding a layer of protection from spammers and hackers who are trying to steal your personal information. If they don't know you're out there, they can't go after you. Go online, and in a search engine such as Yahoo! or Google, type the words "anonymous surfing." You'll find a list of both commercial and free services that provide anonymous surfing. The current free service of favor is Surf Net at http://surfshield.net.[28]

ALSO SEE: "Banking Online" (page 21); "Identity Theft" (page 31); "Bogus Web Sites" (page 102); "Phishing for Your Credit Card Number" (page 110).

[27]At least they can't right now. Who knows what tomorrow will bring?

[28]At least it was at the time I wrote this book; by the time you read this, it may have changed. Such is the nature of the Internet.

Phishing for Your Credit Card Number

THE SCAM

You check your e-mail daily and find a message from somebody named Mike Forrest from AOL support. His message is a dire one: identity thieves are attempting to penetrate AOL and you are *required* to reply to Mike's e-mail and validate your credit card number or face expulsion from the AOL family.

The message scares you—precisely what it's designed to do. You follow Mike's directions explicitly and reply with your credit card number. Literally in seconds, the identity thieves behind the fake e-mail have transmitted your credit card information to Paris, where other thieves will now go on a shopping spree. Your credit card has been compromised, as has your credit reputation. You're in one nasty jam.

In an alternative scenario, Mike's e-mail may contain a link

> **N**ever send information such as credit card numbers, Social Security numbers, or the like in response to an e-mail requesting them. Treat the request as a scam because that's exactly what it is.

with instructions to click it to open an AOL Web site (in truth a clever imitation of an AOL Web site, not a real one). Once clicked open, it asks you to enter your credit card number to validate your identity. The result is the same: your credit card number has been stolen.

Both scenarios are part of a scam called "phishing," a cleverly devised method of persuading or coercing Internet users into divulging sensitive information such as credit card numbers, bank account numbers, and Social Security numbers.

HOW TO SPOT THE SCAM

Understand that AOL or any other reputable Internet service provider (ISP) never asks for sensitive information after your account has been established. Treat any e-mail asking you for this as phony.

Keep tabs on new charges to your account through the Web site maintained by your credit card company. I conduct a daily online check of new charges to my credit card and my wife's. I suggest you do the same; it takes only a couple of minutes. If you see a new charge you didn't make, you're in a good position to cut off other charges to your card before additional damage is done. All major credit card companies allow you to access your personal statement daily.

In any case, your liability by federal law is limited to $50. But when identity thieves latch onto your credit card information, you're in for a year or so of registering complaints, writing letters, pleading with the credit rating agencies, filing reports with the police and FBI, and an entire host of other time-consuming and highly irritating activities.

HOW TO PREVENT THE SCAM

- Never, under any circumstances, send sensitive information such as your credit card number or bank account number in response to an e-mail from somebody you don't know, even though that person represents himself to be from an organization you're dealing with. It pays to make a telephone call to your ISP (or bank or any other company supposedly requesting the information) to verify the request. Or you can contact the ISP or bank through a Web site address you know to be genuine, not the address supplied through the phishing e-mail.

- Whatever you do, don't click a link in the suspect e-mail. That could open your system to hackers, who may then plant some nasty little device on your hard drive and steal all your personal information.

- Before sending sensitive information to any Web site, look for the lock icon in the browser's status bar at the bottom of your screen. It takes the form of a locked padlock. That's your indication of a secure transaction.

- Finally, report suspicious activity to the Federal Trade Commission. Forward the suspect e-mail message to uce@ ftc.gov.

ALSO SEE: "Banking Online" (page 21); "Identity Theft" (page 31); "Bogus Web Sites" (page 102); "Dangerous Spam E-mail" (page 105).

Investments and Home Ownership

The safest way to double your money is to fold it over once and put it in your pocket.

—FRANK MCKINNEY HUBBARD

Besides health and medical frauds, you, as a senior, are most susceptible to investment scams. It's here you'll find the slickest, most persuasive charmers imaginable. Not to mention high-pressure sales types who know how to psychologically twist your arm until you sign on the dotted line. These are guys and gals steeped in the techniques of enticement. Most of them operate with the express purpose of taking money from your pockets in the form of hefty sales commissions.

It's here that seniors, even the most highly educated and sophisticated among us, are vulnerable to doing things we regret the next morning. Things worse than a thousand hangovers, because you can lose piles of money, possibly even all you own.

Financial Planners

THE SCAM

You need a professional to help you plan new investments. You select a financial planner and pay him for his time. He advises you to put your money into certain stocks or mutual funds or annuities. Unbeknownst to you, this guy is receiving a sales commission from every investment you make through him. That's a big no-no. It represents a conflict of interest and, indeed may even be illegal. How can you trust the goat to guard the cabbage patch?

Financial planners who earn commissions from investments they recommend are likely breaking the law. Steer clear of financial planners whose first words to you are "variable annuities."

HOW TO SPOT THE SCAM

There are three almost-sure ways to recognize the scam.

- First, if your financial planner steers you into investing in variable annuities or front-loaded mutual funds, chances are this guy is taking advantage of you because variable annuities and front-loaded mutual funds are where the sales commissions are highest. So his interests precede yours, if yours are even on the table.
- The second way to spot a scam is if he steers you in the direction of investments that will "double your money in ninety days," or any other scheme that smacks of pie-in-the-sky thinking ("Become a millionaire in ten years"; "Turn $1,000 into $10,000 overnight"; "Get a 1,000 percent risk-free return on high-yield bonds.") These are outright frauds in the making. Case in point: Federal prosecutors indicted the owner of a Burbank, California, escrow company for a $100 million financial-planning scam involving over a thousand investors, most of them seniors. Those who bought shares in the company were promised 25 percent return on their investment annually. They were assured the company was buying insurance policies at a discount to be sold later at a higher price when, in fact, no such policies existed. Instead, the company used money from gullible investors to fatten the bank accounts of company owners. Supposedly independent financial planners sold this to innocent investors.
- The third way to spot the scam involves a financial advisor's suggestion to buy art, stamps, Krugerrands, commodities, or any other investment you don't understand. If it's beyond

your area of expertise, chances are you'll lose money on it while he pockets fat sales commissions. Leave such investments to experts who know the ins and outs of the market for specialty financial products.

HOW TO PREVENT THE SCAM

- Deal exclusively with a Certified Financial Planner (CFP). That title assures that your advisor follows the strict code of ethics of the Certified Financial Planner Board of Standards Inc. Of course, that doesn't mean a con artist can't get licensed. It does mean that the risks of having a cheat latch onto your assets are considerably less.
- Double check. After all, it's your money at risk. Don't be too anxious to give it away. A guiding rule, as I mentioned above, is don't invest in anything you don't understand.
- Another guiding rule: Before you plunk down money in any investment, check out complaints against the company (both the financial planner and the company he recommends investing in) with the Better Business Bureau and your state's attorney general or consumer affairs office. And don't forget to check with your state securities regulator to make sure the company you're investing in is registered to sell investments in your state. If your financial planner is trying to sell you anything even remotely suspect, drop him like a sack of concrete from the back of a pickup truck.

ALSO SEE: "Financial Seminars" (page 117); "Investment Schemes" (page 125); "Mutual Funds" (page 133); "Variable Annuities" (page 141).

Financial Seminars

THE SCAM

You receive an invitation in the mail to attend a financial seminar followed by a free steak dinner at a local restaurant. Engraved tickets are enclosed. Hey! Something for nothing. You can't wait to attend.

You do and you may regret it. The least you'll walk away with will be a headache from the pressure put on you by fast-talking salespeople with fancy names such as living trust[29] advisors, senior estate planners, financial specialists, even paralegals. The worst you'll walk away with is a loss of much of what you own.

> There is no such thing as a free steak dinner. The salespeople who sent you that invitation will make you sweat for your hunk of red meat. That free dinner might cost you thousands of dollars.

The steak dinner isn't free; expect to pay sometime. As I've said before in this book, there is no free lunch (or dinner, as it

---

[29]A living trust is a legal means of assuring that your property and assets are transferred to your heirs according to your wishes. It differs from a will in several respects, the primary difference being that a will is subject to probate, a living trust isn't.

were). The people handing out the steak dinner are in business to sell you financial products, and the shaky financial products they often sell leave you losing money while paying the weasels handsome sales commissions.

Under the guise of helping you improve the performance of your investment portfolio, these slick sales types dig deep to uncover the specific assets you own—cash, bonds, stocks, annuities, and so on. They are now in a position to recommend investments in other financial products "that will double, even triple the returns you're currently earning *without any additional risk.*" Wow! You are suitably impressed. The more you own, the higher the applied pressure.

A second meeting follows in which the salesperson persuades you to cash in your paid-up annuities, your IRAs, your stocks and bonds—in short, everything you own, sometimes even your home—and invest in the shaky financial products he's representing. You do, and six months later you wake up one morning to find the company you invested in has gone bankrupt. You lose 90 percent of everything you own, while the salesman is tending his thirty-foot sailboat in the Bahamas.

HOW TO SPOT THE SCAM

At the very least, before you sit down for your "free" steak dinner, the financial advisors paying for the feast will require you to provide contact information. In which case expect a follow-up call within a few days, soliciting a free consultation designed to develop your own personalized financial plan. (See appendix A, page 227, where I describe a similar experience that happened to me.) The scenario then develops along the lines I mentioned above. The steak dinner itself should alert you to a high-pressure sell for possibly shaky investments. Ignore the invitation; you don't need the grief. Besides, you don't still eat red meat, do you?

HOW TO PREVENT THE SCAM

California's Department of Corporations (http://www.corp.ca.gov or call toll-free 1-866-275-2677) has developed a checklist you can use at one of these so-called financial seminars to help you avoid being taken. It advises:

- Never make a decision about investing at the first meeting. Instead, review the salesman's recommendations with a lawyer, accountant, or personal friend familiar with contracts and investments who can provide competent advice.
- Get copies of all documents you're expected to sign and review them carefully to assure they match what the salesman told you. Do not sign on the dotted line until you've had a chance to review them *away* from the presence of the salesman.
- Ask the salesman if he's licensed by your state to sell securities. But just to make sure, call your state consumer affairs office and verify it.
- Don't be impressed by fancy titles such as senior estate planner. Even a pig can call itself a tiger if it wants. (This last sentence didn't come from the Department of Corporations. Just adding my personal flavor.)
- Beware of words such as "guaranteed," "bonded," "risk free," "insured," "free of charge." These claims should alert you to a probable scam.
- Better yet (my recommendation), don't attend the financial seminar to begin with. Why ask for trouble? If you still insist

on eating red meat, buy your own steak dinner. It's a good way to avoid indigestion.

- Whatever you decide to do, never, never reveal how much you own of any investment (real estate, stock, bonds, cash, etc.). You will be under pressure to do so. Instead, take the advice of former president Reagan's wife Nancy: Just say no.

ALSO SEE: "Financial Planners" (page 114); "Investment Schemes" (page 125); "Mutual Funds" (page 133); "Variable Annuities" (page 141).

Home Loans

THE SCAM

You're living on Social Security and a small annuity. Rising prices are causing you to make some unpleasant choices between eating three meals a day or taking your prescribed drugs.[30] All too many lenders are waiting for you to make yourself known so they can "help you with your problem." Here are just a few of the home-loan scams they've devised to take some or all of your money[31]:

Crooked lenders know a dozen ways to bamboozle you into taking out home loans you don't need. And even if you do need them, there are cheaper ways to lay your hands on some dough. Much cheaper ways.

Equity Stripping

You run across an ad in the paper advertising favorable mortgage loan rates, and you call. A persuasive lender talks you into padding

---

[30]Unfortunately, not an uncommon occurrence among seniors too poor to afford both.

[31]Go to the Federal Trade Commision's Web site http://www.ftc.gov/bcp/conline/pubs/homes/eqscams.htm.

your monthly income on the loan application so you can be eligible for the loan. You're so desperate you're not thinking straight, so you go along with the scheme. The loan goes through and the monthly payments are so high you can't meet them. The lending institution forecloses. You're out on the street and the equity you've built up in the home over the years has been stripped away by the lender.

Balloon Payment

You're having trouble meeting your monthly mortgage payment. A lender helps you refinance the loan so that you can meet the monthly payment. You're happy she was there to help you until the loan period is up, when you're shocked to discover you're left with a large balloon payment of the principal and accumulated interest. It's beyond your ability to pay. The lender forecloses.

Loan Flipping

A lender persuades you to refinance your mortgage with lower monthly payments so you have money left over for the down payment on a new car. You buy the car and make the first few payments on the mortgage. Everything is fine. Tight but fine. The lender now suggests that you finance the purchase of a timeshare on Hilton Head Island with another refinancing of your home. Best of all worlds: your monthly payments will be even lower. Wow! You go along, thinking it's a great idea. What the lender has done is refinance, or "flip" over your original loan and added higher interest rates for the new loan (the payments still appear lower, because there are more of them). And, to add insult to injury, you have to pay a prepayment penalty to retire the old loan. What you've done is stretch the horizon of your debt such that it's now almost never-ending. Not too bad if you live to be 125; otherwise not such a good deal. If you default on the loan, well, you know what to expect, don't you?

Deed Stripping

You're in danger of being foreclosed and you're frantic to find a way out. An oily lender talks you into refinancing and signing over to him the deed to your home. He leaves you with the distinct impression that it's just a ploy to prevent the bank from foreclosing on your loan. The slimeball tells you that the bank can't foreclose if the deed isn't in your name. You're happy you finally found a lender who thinks more about his customers than himself. Think again. If you agree to this blatant attempt to rob you, you're no longer a homeowner, simply a tenant. The lender owns the home and all the equity you put into it. If you can't make the rent payments, he has the right to evict you, and don't for one New York minute think he won't.

HOW TO SPOT THE SCAM

In every example shown above, the bottom line is that you have added debt. The monthly payments may be lower but the end result is that the debt has to be serviced, so its time frame is extended. Consequently you should ask yourself two questions before you take on more debt: (1) How much more is the refinancing going to cost in terms of additional debt? (2) Will I be able to make the payments?

HOW TO PREVENT THE SCAM

Here is a list of do's and don'ts:

- Don't panic if you're in a tight financial spot. Step back and take a few deep breaths. I know this is easier to say than do, but it's necessary that you think your way out of the problem, and that takes a clear head.
- Never sign a loan agreement you don't fully understand. Read everything in the loan contract carefully. Best of all worlds, pay a lawyer to review it. It may cost you a few dollars up front but save you thousands later, and maybe even your home.
- Nail down the monthly payment and don't agree to refinance unless you can comfortably meet that payment. Before you sign, make sure you know all the associated costs. If you're billed for something you think is wrong, speak up, challenge it. Don't let anybody push you around. The law is on your side, and believe me, the courts and police despise con artist lowlifes who prey on seniors even more than you do.
- Maintain detailed records of all refinancing charges. Keep copies of all documents involved in the transaction along with the canceled checks.
- Finally, never, never hand over the deed to your property or sign a quit claim[32] to it as long as you own the home. Not for any reason.

ALSO SEE: "Reverse Mortgages" (page 138).

---

[32]A quit claim is a form signing over the ownership of your property to another person or organization.

Investment Schemes

THE SCAM

You're approached by an insurance broker, somebody you know and have done business with. She takes you aside and excitedly tells you about an investment opportunity in promissory notes,[33] the hottest thing going. She claims it will deliver a high and steady annual stream of interest payments to the tune of 15 percent of your investment.

It sure sounds lucrative, and the nice part is that the notes are secured, meaning they're backed by company collateral.[34] Sounds foolproof. Besides, you believe the lady because

> **B**eware of investing in any financial instrument you've never heard of, like prime bank notes and cell phone contracts. You're sure to get stung. Even the experts shy away from them.

[33]Short-term loans that companies float to finance their daily operations. They pay a fixed rate of return to individuals and companies lending the money.

[34]Hard assets such as cash, notes, inventory, physical property, machinery, and equipment.

you've done business with her for five years and you trust her judgment. Your comfort level is high.

You buy ten grand worth of promissory notes and sit back and watch the interest payments flow in. But, unexpectedly, the interest stream dries out in three months. The issuing company has declared bankruptcy, and you're dismayed to realize your ten grand just got washed down the drain. You may—repeat may—get thirty cents on the dollar back when a bankruptcy court adjudicates disposition of company assets, but don't count on it. And even that possibility may take many, many years. What a bummer.

HOW TO SPOT THE SCAM

The very fact that a company is willing to pay 15 percent for a debt instrument when the going market rate for 12-month investments is 4 percent tells you the company is desperate for cash. And any company desperate for cash is usually struggling to survive. This, it turns out, was your typical pie-in-the-sky investment scheme, the kind that's scammed untold numbers of seniors.

The same can be said for a variety of "exciting" investment products such as high-yield investments, prime bank notes, options, investment trusts, ATM and pay phone contracts, blind pool investments, and viatical settlements.[35] Don't worry about what those terms mean; just be on the lookout for them, because they're either outright frauds or ventures so risky that your invested capital can disappear virtually overnight. If you want to learn more about these and other risky investments, go online to

[35]This one deserves explanation because it's so ghoulish. Viatical settlements are based on buying heavily discounted life insurance policies from people who are dying and then collecting the full amount after their deaths. It started ten years ago when dying AIDS patients needed money to see them through their remaining months.

http://www.nasaa.org, the Web site of North American Securities Administrators Association (NASAA).

HOW TO PREVENT THE SCAM

- Suspect any investment that veers from traditional investments such as stocks, bonds, treasuries, and bank certificates of deposit. Nine times out of ten, these investment schemes were designed by hucksters to scam innocent folks such as you out of your money. Leave those kind of investments to financial experts who have the expertise to handle them. Incidentally, you'll find only a relative handful of professional investors willing to risk their money on such fanciful schemes. Most professionals, aware of the shaky foundation of these non-traditional investment schemes, shun them. You should, too.

- You should also be aware that most securities must be registered by your state securities regulator. So ask your insurance broker if the product she's selling (which, incidentally, may line her pockets with a whopping 40 percent sales commission) is registered with the state, and ask her if she's licensed to sell securities. But be aware that in the case of the promissory notes described in the example above, securities are normally exempt from licensing requirements if their maturities[36] are nine months or less.

ALSO SEE: "Financial Planners" (page 114); "Financial Seminars" (page 117); "Living Wills" (page 72); "Mutual Funds" (page 133); "Variable Annuities" (page 141).

[36]The time period you hold the investment.

Phony IRS Letters

THE SCAM

You're an elderly gentleman who takes pride in your determination to support the American government by paying your taxes on time and in full. Never once have you tried to cheat Uncle Sam.

You receive a letter in the mail from the IRS stating that unless you fill out the enclosed IRS Form W-9095[37] and fax it to the IRS, your bank will begin withholding taxes on your account and automatically forward them to the IRS. You have never had taxes withheld on the interest you earned in your money

> Anytime you receive a letter from the IRS and it just doesn't sound right, call the local IRS office and verify information contained in the letter. This is the quickest way to expose a swindle.

market account or certificates of deposit (CDs). Instead, you paid taxes every quarter by estimating the amount. You prefer it that way; it's simple and direct.

[37]Obviously not a real IRS form but one made up by scammers to look something like a genuine form.

You fill out the form, which includes your bank account routing and account numbers and your Social Security number, and you fax it into the number provided. You've just handed information over to scammers who will drain your bank accounts and obtain credit cards in your name.

HOW TO SPOT THE SCAM

It is rare that the IRS will send out such a letter, and then it's only done in cases where the taxpayer has not reported his or her interest income. If you've been paying your taxes on time and in full, this letter should tip you off to a scam.

HOW TO PREVENT THE SCAM

You can't stop the crooks from trying to defraud you, but you can make sure this egregious scam doesn't work. Take the following precautions:

- Question the veracity of every such letter you receive, not only from the IRS, but from any city, county, state, or federal agency. Do not automatically assume it's genuine, even if the letter looks official. Remember, given today's printing technology, anybody with a computer and a printer can knock out fake stationery that looks like the real thing.
- If you receive such a letter and you're still unsure, call the agency it purportedly came from and verify its authenticity. In the case of the IRS letter, you have the option of calling your bank or the IRS.
- If you've already been scammed, call the Treasury Inspector General's Hotline at 1-800-366-4484.

Mechanic's Lien

THE SCAM

You're a senior couple who retired fifteen years ago and bought a new home. It's held up pretty well through the years, except the wood on the back deck is now rotting out and you've decided to replace it. You hire a general contractor, and he buys the lumber and nails and hires two helpers to tear down the old deck and build the a new one. Unfortunately the general contractor goes bankrupt shortly afterward. Three months later you receive a bill from a local lumberyard for the lumber used in your deck. Apparently the general contractor never paid the lumberyard. You're shocked to discover you're liable for the bill despite having paid the general contractor for the job.

> If a general contractor remodeling your home defaults on payments to a subcontractor or supplier, you may be liable for payment even if you paid the contractor in full. Lien wavers can protect you.

HOW TO SPOT THE SCAM

Individual state laws allow subcontractors or suppliers to file liens *against your home* for payment when they've been stiffed by a general contractor, even when the homeowner has paid the general contractor in full for services rendered. Subcontractors or suppliers furnishing services or materials for construction or remodeling of your home are legally entitled to the value of the services or materials provided. This could tie up the ownership of your home for months or years to come until the courts sort out the mess.

Obviously you're not going to know if the general contractor is paying his bills unless you check with his subcontractors or suppliers, so you're in the dark. The best way to handle this situation is by taking the preventive steps shown below.

HOW TO PREVENT THE SCAM

- You can prevent having a lien filed against your property by obtaining a legal instrument called a lien waiver. When you hire someone to build or remodel your home, don't pay the contractor or anyone else until you receive a waiver from each subcontractor or supplier involved in the job.
- Obviously, you're not going to go to this trouble for every nickel-and-dime improvement made, but when you're talking thousands of dollars, and you're unsure about the financial stability of the general contractor, prudence dictates that you protect yourself through lien waivers. For example, if a new general contractor is building your house, you may want lien

waivers since the probability of a new business failing is high.

- When asking for lien waivers, it's best to have a lawyer handle the transactions.

ALSO SEE: "Home Repairs" (page 152).

Mutual Funds

THE SCAM

A bank certificate of deposit worth $100,000 comes due, and you and your wife, now in your late fifties, are interested in placing the money in the stock market. You don't want stocks that are excessively risky like dot-com companies, but stocks with some reasonable expectation of growth over a horizon of ten

Before investing your hard-earned money in a mutual fund, check out the advice and recommendations in the annual mutual funds issue of *Consumer Reports*. It could save you a bunch of money.

years. And you don't want to risk all your money on a single company, so you decide to purchase mutual funds.

You approach your stockbroker—or financial advisor, investment planner, whatever else they're called nowadays—and ask for her assistance. She steers you to a mutual fund that charges 5.5 percent up front with annual maintenance fees running 1.5 percent annually. Your out-of-pocket cost is $5,500 up front and about $1,500 per year for fund upkeep. You may regret your decision when you discover other mutual funds that are equally good investments without up-front costs and with lower annual fees.

HOW TO SPOT THE SCAM

You've been sold what's called a front-end-load mutual fund. That's because the mutual fund industry has been turning more and more to aggressive financial advisors or brokers to sell their products, and those hungry boys and girls need to earn their fat commissions. The load is what they charge up front. Furthermore, you may pay a 12b-1 fee, which covers the fund's costs of marketing and advertising. You can buy mutual funds without paying these exorbitant expenses.

HOW TO PREVENT THE SCAM

- Buy no-load mutual funds directly from mutual fund companies. You won't pay up-front sales commissions because there aren't any financial advisors or brokers involved in the transaction. According to *Consumer Reports,* no-load mutual funds tend to either equal or outperform front-end-load funds.[38] So don't let anybody tell you that front-end-load funds have higher returns than no-load funds. Some do, but many do not. And no-load mutual fund annual expenses can run considerably less, as low as 0.25 percent. Compare that to the front-end-load mutual fund you bought. On that hundred grand you're investing, you'll save a bundle: $5,500 up front and $1,500 per year in fund expenses.

[38]March, 2004, pages 12–16.

- Read the annual mutual funds issue of *Consumer Reports* every year. It contains loads of information to steer you in the right direction.
- Check online at http://www.morningstar.com, an independent authority that rates mutual funds. Its Web site contains valuable and easy-to-understand primers on investing.

ALSO SEE: "Financial Planners" (page 114); "Financial Seminars" (page 117); "Investment Schemes" (page 125); "Variable Annuities" (page 141).

Property Tax

THE SCAM

You notice an ad in the local newspaper from some group called the County Tax Reduction Organization informing you that you have the right to apply for a senior homestead exemption. You're hot for that because senior homestead status means a significant reduction in property taxes. All you have to do is fill out an application and mail in a fee of $100.

The advertisement

> Solicitations for money in the mail from government agencies (city, county, state) usually turn out to be bogus. Call the appropriate agency to verify the claim. Chances are they're phony.

certainly looks official. You assume it's from the county, so you send in the fee, and soon enough your homestead exemption goes through. You're elated. What you don't know is that the ad that looked official has nothing to do with the county government. Rather, it's a private corporation with a name that makes you associate it with county government. You can get senior homestead exemption for free by filing with the county's property tax office. You've been bilked for a hundred bucks.

HOW TO SPOT THE SCAM

Question any solicitation that requests a fee and couples it with a government service. That's something that should make you automatically suspicious.

Call me distrustful, but whenever I receive any solicitation by phone, mail, fax, or e-mail, and whoever is pitching something asks for money, I *never* respond. Let's face it: if whatever they're peddling is so valuable, they won't need to promote it; consumers will flock to them. Am I missing out on something valuable? Possibly, but ninety-nine times out of a hundred it's a scam and a waste of my time.

HOW TO PREVENT THE SCAM

Here, like in other scams involving so-called government agencies, your good old horse sense counts. Use the following guidelines:

- Normally, a government-granted status like a senior homestead exemption is granted by the county without charging fees. The best bet is to call the county tax office and find out before you throw away your money on solicitations.
- Such a solicitation may in fact be illegal since most counties and states have trade practices acts that prohibit such fraudulent commerce. Contact your county district attorney's office if you suspect a scam.

Reverse Mortgages

THE SCAM

You and your wife have been living in the same house now for almost thirty years. Unfortunately, the cost of living has caught up with you and outpaced your ability to provide for yourselves. You're now in a position where it will be necessary to borrow money to meet daily expenses.

An ad over talk radio catches your attention. Lenders propose that you apply for a reverse mortgage and cash in on the home equity you've built up over the years. That sounds like a winner, and you call a toll-free 1-800 number and arrange for a lender to visit you.

Reverse mortgages are a great way for elderly people to receive an infusion of badly needed cash, provided they deal with honest brokers. Find out from HUD which are the best in your area.

She does and explains that a reverse mortgage enables you and your wife, the homeowners, to borrow against the value of your home. You can elect to receive payments from the lender on a monthly basis, in a lump sum, or as a line of credit. Repayments are not required while you and your wife live in your home. The lender recovers its loan plus interest from the sale of the home when you and your wife move out or die.

This is the answer to your prayers. The saleslady signs you up; you pay a hefty fee of 10 percent to apply (in round numbers, $7,500), but you think it's worthwhile.

The scam is that no legitimate lender will require you to pay a loan application fee when applying for a reverse mortgage, at least not of that magnitude. You've just lost $7,500.

HOW TO SPOT THE SCAM

Any lender charging you an application fee for what the U.S. Department of Housing and Urban Development (HUD) will mail you for free is an outright crook. Don't pay it. You can get a loan application with instructions at no cost from HUD.

HOW TO PREVENT THE SCAM

To keep from getting ripped off in the reverse mortgage process, you need to understand some fundamentals:

- Your best bet is a loan made by a bank, mortgage company, or some other lender that's backed by the U.S. Government through a federally insured Home Equity Conversion Mortgage (HECM). HECM loans often provide much greater loan advances than other reverse mortgages and assure that lenders comply with such laws as the federal Truth in Lending Act.
- You do not surrender ownership of your home. It is still your home and will remain so until you die or sell the home.

- The lender does not impose any conditions on what you do with the loan. That's entirely your decision.
- Your credit rating does not affect the lender's decision about granting the loan. The only prerequisites involve your age (HUD specifies a minimum age of sixty-two), condition of the property, and home value.
- When you and your wife die, your heirs will inherit the home and the equity you have in it. Of course, they will have to retire the reverse mortgage loan.

ALSO SEE: "Home Loans" (page 121).

Variable Annuities

THE SCAM

Every year thousands of seniors are conned by slick-talking financial advisors[39] who push them into purchasing variable annuities. You know the type of salespeople I'm referring to: fast-talking wolves who are glib enough to talk seniors like you and me into cashing out every asset we own, then jumping into investments they claim will double our money and make us millionaires practically over-

> Variable annuities are the poster boy for avaricious salespeople who place their interests above yours. Way above. More seniors get screwed buying this financial product than any other.

night. Investments that can, in the real world, send even moderately affluent seniors scrambling to the bank or to their kids, borrowing money to pay their food and pharmacy bills, because annuity surrender fees have eaten up their available cash.

---

[39]Once called stockbrokers, now called by fancy names such as financial advisors and investment counselors. Those who prey on seniors would be more aptly named wolves.

Incidentally, variable annuities are joined at the hip with, and based on, investment products such as stocks and bonds. The annuity's rate of return generally depends on how well the insurance company's portfolios of stocks and bonds fare in the open market. Fixed annuities, by contrast are not based on any specific investment product. Their return is predicated on what the insurance company issuing the annuity promised to pay.

Why do these hungry wolves push variable annuities so much? Because that's where sales commissions are highest. Many of them are downright outrageous. If you think I'm exaggerating, ask Clark Howard, arguably the country's number one consumer advocate, who has information on variable annuity scams at his Web site (http://www.clarkhoward.com). Or listen to consumer writer Jane Bryant Quinn, who says variable annuities are products she "dreams of blowing to smithereens."[40]

Annuity salesmen may promise the variable annuity they're peddling is "guaranteed" to return your original invested principle, even if the insurance company isn't profitable. But over time if a company isn't profitable, it will ultimately go belly up. Then what happens to your money? Today's glib salesmen may tell you that the insurance company establishes an escrow account to protect your investment. However, in the case of a bankruptcy, who knows when—and if—you will get your money back? I certainly don't. Hey, like you, I'm from the generation that was born during the Great Depression and schooled by its survivors. And I've seen and heard untold numbers of horror stories of companies screwing over their pensioners and stock-

---

[40]Ms. Quinn does qualify that statement, however, by stating there are some acceptable variable annuities. To find out more, go online to Money Bulletin at http://www.moneybulletin.com/New/14-Feb-2005.shtml.

holders (anybody ever hear of Enron?). Enough not to have faith in a "guarantee." In the final analysis, there just ain't any such animal.

Unfortunately, investment wolves do not always work for fly-by-night outfits. Some of them are employees of the largest and most prestigious financial institutions in the country. For example, in 2004 the National Association of Security Dealers (NASD) ordered Prudential Equity Group to refund $9.5 million to customers for selling variable annuities and other annuities that violated New York state law and NASD rules. It slapped the company with a $2 million fine.

In the same year, the NASD charged Waddell & Reed Inc. for recommending 6,700 possibly unsuitable variable annuity switches (trading existing paid-up annuities for new variable annuities), thereby adding new sales commissions and surrender fees. These exchanges cost customers, many of them seniors, nearly $10 million. According to the NASD, 1,400 of the customers involved could have lost money by switching policies.

HOW TO SPOT THE SCAM

Stories about financial rip-offs of seniors abound. They're reported almost daily in the press and over talk radio, and frequently enough on television to make us all aware of the shark-infested[41] waters of financial advice, particularly those featuring variable annuities.

But if you're on information overload, as so many people are today, and you're not in tune with daily happenings in the finan-

---

[41]I know, I know. I switched metaphors. From wolves to sharks. But it seemed to fit.

cial community, here are a few tips that will allow you to spot an approaching variable annuity scam:

- If the first words out of your financial advisor's mouth are "variable annuities," particularly before he's had an opportunity to review your personal financial situation, hang up the phone or walk out of his office. This guy does not have your interests at heart. His goal is socking it to you to earn himself a juicy sales commission.
- Fly-by-night financial firms are generally easy to spot: people in sleazy offices peddling unknown financial products. Seniors can usually see these wolves coming and are savvy enough to avoid them (usually, but not always). Fly-by-nighters aren't the problem. Instead, seniors need to beware of impressive-appearing financial advisors in impressive offices located in impressive office buildings. Most of us (me included) tend to let their guard down in the face of money and power and make the erroneous assumption they equate to fair play. They don't. You're on your own.
- If your financial advisor tries to overwhelm you with technical financial jargon and impressive personalized computerized reports it takes a Philadelphia lawyer to understand, watch out. That's a sign he's covering up something he doesn't want you to see—usually obscenely fat commissions flying out of your pocketbook and into his.

HOW TO PREVENT THE SCAM

- First, and most important, *never,* repeat *never,* make a decision while you're in a financial advisor's office or on the phone with him. Get the proposal in writing. Always. Take the material home and discuss it with your spouse. Then ask your grown kids to look it over. Ask your banker to review it. If you're fortunate enough to know somebody trustworthy in the financial community like a CPA or lawyer, ask him or her to examine the proposal with a critical eye.

- Assure the proposal is in line with your financial goals. If your goal is preservation of capital, the investments planned for you should meet that important criterion.

- Keep these facts well in mind: Moving into variable annuities means you probably will lose money up front for sales commissions, along with stiff annual maintenance expenses. Not to mention the taxes you'll pay when you cash in other investments like paid-up annuities or IRAs to buy the variable annuity. It almost certainly will mean that your invested capital will not be available to you for a few years without paying a hefty surrender fee. (Author's note: I wrote an article on my personal experience with a large, national financial institution. It's reprinted in appendix A.)

ALSO SEE: "Financial Planners" (page 114); "Financial Seminars" (page 117); "Investment Schemes" (page 125); "Mutual Funds" (page 133).

Repairs

> **People need good lies. There are too many bad ones.**
>
> **—KURT VONNEGUT, JR.**

Our material possessions, like our bodies, break down over time. The most expensive of those possessions traditionally are your home and your car. And it's here that scammers prey on vulnerable seniors because when it comes to repairs, most of us are technological dummies. So read on and discover the more common scams and how to keep from being fleeced by tradesmen.

Car Repairs

THE SCAM

Your seven-year-old-Honda finally breaks down and you use your AAA membership to haul the car to a local garage. You consider yourself fortunate because other than routine mainte-nance and tire and battery changes, the car has never broken down. Until now.

The mechanic gives you the bad news. Your Honda needs a new transmission. Cost: three grand. Your knees suddenly feel weak and you plop down on the nearest chair in the garage's waiting room. Since you're liv-ing on a fixed income, any large and unex-pected expenditure of money is as welcome as a coiled rattlesnake in the family room.

> Anybody who has ever owned a car knows how difficult it is to find a reliable mechanic when your car breaks down. Get competing bids until you find a mechanic who won't scam you.

Your dear wife of forty years doesn't react as emotionally as you. She wants a second opinion, reasoning that it should work here as well as it does when a doctor gives you an unfavorable diagnosis and you want it confirmed. She calls a few friends and gets the name of a repair shop two of those friends have used for the past half-dozen years. You arrange to have the Honda transported to that repair shop. The mechanic there says the transmission doesn't need to be replaced, just repaired. He fixes it and you drive away happy. Cost: $285. Savings: $3,000 − $285 = $2,715.

HOW TO SPOT THE SCAM

Few of us are auto mechanics. We're at the mercy of mechanics who want to cheat us. And don't believe for a minute that seniors don't make tempting targets to many unscrupulous mechanics lying in wait for such mechanically-deficient patsies.

If you're unsure about what to do in the face of an expensive diagnosis, do what the senior's wife did: get another opinion. Or find a service, an objective third party, that will check the car out for you. At a fee, of course. But that fee might save you thousands of dollars. Go online and look up car repair scams and you'll find many such services. (One such service is listed under "Car Repairs" in appendix B, page 240.)

Some state lemon laws require dealers to provide a refund or replacement should your car continually break down or the same problem continue to recur. Contact The Center for Auto Safety at http://www.autosafety.org or call them at 1-202-328-7700 to find out about your state's lemon laws. Or contact your state's consumer affairs department for further information.

HOW TO PREVENT THE SCAM

- Like the senior's wife in the example above, ask friends and associates for the names of repair shops they've dealt with.
- Failing that, look for shops with service technicians who are certified by the National Institute for Automotive Service Excellence (ASE) (see "Car Repairs" [page 240 in appendix B]).
- Check with the Better Business Bureau (BBB). If the repair shop is a member of the BBB and has no complaints listed against it, you've at least located a mechanic who knows what he's doing. (Just remember, the BBB deals with quality of service, not what customers pay. So the recommended car mechanic may be expensive.)
- Describe the problem to the mechanic and make sure you get an estimate in writing.
- The kind of mechanic you want to deal with will explain the repair and tell you what has to be done. She will also save the old parts taken from your car for your inspection. If you still have suspicions, ask another mechanic to check the parts she gave you.
- Get a written guarantee in case the repair doesn't work. Faulty repairs are more commonplace than you can imagine.
- When you're getting your oil changed in a repair shop that sells tires, make sure you check your cold tire pressure before you hand over the car. Then before you drive away, check the cold tire pressure again. If you find the tires deflated after the oil change, you're onto a scam. Too many greedy shop managers let air out of your tires without telling you. If they're discovered, they'll claim softer tire pressure equates to a softer ride. What it really does is make your

tires wear out faster. Then guess who will sell you replacement tires. If you catch a scoundrel doing it, never go back to his shop again, and make sure you report the shop to the BBB and your state's consumer affairs office.

- If you feel your car is a lemon, take the following precautions:
  - Keep copies of each repair order, showing dates of service and repairs made.
  - Contact the manufacturer through the address in your car's manual. Send the manufacturer a registered letter, return receipt requested, describing the problems.
  - Read about similar problems with your car model on the message board at http://www.safetyforum.com. This Web site lists lemons that owners have had to deal with. A history of similar complaints about your car provides further ammunition when you file your claim for replacement or reimbursement.

Home Repairs

THE SCAM

Somebody knocks on your door. When you answer, a man dressed in work clothes tells you he's a contractor on the way from a job and he noticed that your brick front porch is sagging to one side. You accompany him outside to examine the damage, but you don't see it. The contractor says that's because you have an untrained eye.

C hances are the contractor who knocks on your door and says he was driving by and spotted something wrong with your home is a phony. Legitimate contractors don't solicit work this way. Be suspicious.

He, on the other hand, can detect a budding problem because that's his business. He adds that the damaged porch is a safety hazard and is in violation of county building codes. This alarms you and you authorize him to repair the sagging brick porch. He "repairs" the porch and presents you with a bill for $2,000. You gladly pay, if only not to be in violation of the law. What you don't know is that there was never anything wrong with your porch; the contractor just went through the motions of repairing it. You've been royally scammed.

HOW TO SPOT THE SCAM

There are certain signs that should tip you off to the presence of a home-repair scam in the making:

- A contractor, or somebody who purports to be one, solicits your business without being asked. He tells you, as in the above example, that he was just passing by on the way from a job and noticed a structural problem in your home. The tip-off is that door-to-door solicitation isn't something that's usual and expected in contracting work.
- The contractor doesn't have a business card, or if he has one, it doesn't contain his work address and telephone number. Or if it does, you can't find it in either the white pages or the yellow pages of your phone book.
- He's reluctant to give you a written estimate.
- He pressures you to begin the work immediately, citing imminent damage to your home or violations of the building code. Or he attempts to frighten you, stressing the possibility of somebody being hurt by your neglect to fix the problem. Somebody who will then sue you for all you own in this world.
- He requires a large down payment. Personally, I *never* pay anything in advance for home repair, and you should consider adopting the same principle.

HOW TO PREVENT THE SCAM

- First and most important, don't contract for any home repairs without first obtaining three or more estimates. You'll uncover two critical pieces of information: (1) Is there a problem to begin with? Surely, out of the three or more estimates you obtain, at least one honest contractor (yes, there is such an animal but it's on the list of species plunging toward extinction) will tell you if nothing is wrong and the repair is unnecessary. (2) If there is a problem, how much does the repair cost? Don't be surprised if estimates vary as much as 100 percent. But if one of the bids is $2,000 and the other two cluster around $1,000, you'll know the guy who came in at $2,000 is trying to bilk you.

- When you select a contractor, ask to see his state and county licenses authorizing him to do home repair work. Also check to make sure he's properly insured. If he's repairing your roof, for example, and one of his workmen falls off it, you're legally liable if the contractor doesn't have insurance. This is a particularly big issue today because so much home contracting work is done by illegal aliens, many of whom don't have insurance. And illegal alien or not, if there's an accident and the contractor doesn't have insurance, you're paying the medical bills.

- Assure that start and finish dates are clearly written in the contract—speaking of which, make sure there is a written contract to prevent any misunderstandings. Verbal contracts often result in disputes, as both sides often remember a promise differently.

ALSO SEE: "Door-to-Door Salesmen" *(page 176).*

Romance, Charities, and Entertainment

It is human nature to think wisely and act foolishly.

—ANATOLE FRANCE

What's more aggravating than spending thousands of dollars on a vacation only to have it ruined by dirty hotel rooms and poor service? Or a cruise ship that scams you into accepting a lower-level cabin than you paid for? Or searching for a new sweetheart only to find that he or she's swindled you to the tune of thousands of dollars?

The topics in this section show you how to avoid these common scams.

Charities

THE SCAM

You're shopping at your local mall. In the atrium you spot a table under a large banner that reads "Hurricane Relief Fund of the Americas." Behind the table are several poster-size pictures of teary-eyed children hovering in ragged clothes, the clear implication being that these unfortunate tykes have been left homeless by Katrina or other hurricane disasters and need immediate help to sustain the basic necessities of life.

> Fake charities are springing up everywhere, many of them with names that sound like legitimate charities. A sound rule is to "check, not accept" until you've verified the charity's legitimacy.

Your heart goes out. You approach the table staffed by a pair of attractive young women who smile warmly when they see you. They are wearing blue-and-white uniforms similar to what is worn by United Nations relief workers.

The women should smile because they recognize a sympathetic face when they see one, and you're about to get scammed. There is no such organization as Hurricane Relief Fund of the Americas, and the two attractive young women, dressed in their fake UN outfits, are con artists who will use your contribution, along with what other victims hand out, to buy Versace gowns, Prada handbags, Gucci sunglasses, and vacations in the Virgin Islands.

Here's another example: You're sitting at home when the doorbell rings. You answer the door to find a polite young man dressed conservatively and selling magazine subscriptions. Because you like to support youth in all its causes, you buy three subscriptions from him under the assumption that the proceeds go to charity. Aren't you surprised when you later discover the young man works for a commercial organization, not a charity, and that your money is going directly into the coffers of a for-profit corporation?

HOW TO SPOT THE SCAM

Charity scams are among the most difficult of all scams to spot because you're emotionally blinded by the need of desperate people. The scammers often concoct fake names that approximate known relief agencies so that you associate their charities with high-profile relief efforts. For example, one scammer might call his fake charity "United National Children's Support Effort," a fake agency the scammer hopes you will associate with the United Nations.

Because of the difficulty of identifying a genuine charity, prevention is the best cure. Follow the steps listed below.

HOW TO PREVENT THE SCAM

If you see a charity you'd like to contribute to, you should:

- Request the home address and phone number of the charity and its registration number. Any hesitation from the person soliciting will alert you to a potential scam. If you're suspicious, don't contribute then and there, and check on the charity's authenticity. If the organization is unfamiliar to you or if you're just unsure, inquire with the Better Business Bureau's Wise Giving Alliance. The Alliance maintains a registry of several hundred national charitable organizations. Call them at 1-703-276-0100 or visit their Web site at http://www.give.org.

- Never make a donation in cash. Instead, make out a bank check to the name of the charity, not the person soliciting your help. Don't forget to get a receipt for tax purposes. Of course, there still is some risk in writing a check if you're not familiar with the charity. Do your homework as described in the previous steps *before* you write the check.

- If the charity presses you to contribute without delay, your suspicions should be aroused.

- Ignore e-mail pleas for charitable giving. Legitimate charities do not usually solicit by e-mail.

- If solicitations come by phone, ask the requesting party to send you information by regular mail. This usually separates the real charities from the poseurs. When the information arrives, do your due diligence to verify if it's legitimate.

- Simply give to a local charitable organization you're familiar with, such as your local church, synagogue, mosque, or children's shelter. That way you're sure the money will be put to good use.

Lonely Hearts

THE SCAM

Your wife of forty-five years died a year ago. Your kids live on the other side of the country, and you have few friends because you and your wife kept pretty much to yourselves. You're now desperately lonely and emotionally fragile. You've let your appearance deteriorate: you shave only once a week, your clothes are wrinkled and dirty. You just don't care anymore.

When you meet your new sweetheart through an ad in the paper or online, you're risking losing your heart to a con artist who will take thousands of your dollars and run.

You decide enough is enough. You answer an ad in a local lonely hearts newsletter and arrange to meet a widow for a cup of coffee. You're excited and take great care in dressing and grooming yourself appropriately for the occasion.

The widow and you really hit it off. You date her frequently. When you're not with her, you find your mind drifting back to memories of your last date with the lady. You can't get her out of your mind.

After a couple of months of dating she suddenly stops returning your telephone calls. You're devastated and in a near panic. You rush to her apartment and she lets you in with obvious reluctance. What's wrong? You ask. She tells you she's just received some terrible news. Her sister, who retired from Texas to Mexico, is dying and can't use Medicaid where she lives. She's also in no condition to travel back to Texas to receive a free surgical procedure. She needs $50,000 for an operation that could save her life.

Your heart goes out to the poor woman's sister. Besides, you're crazy about your new darling; you don't think you can live without her. You tell her you'll loan her the money. She flies into your arms and everything in your world is okay again.

That is, until the check clears your bank. She vanishes and you're alarmed; you report her disappearance to the police. After an investigation, the police tell you the widow defrauded you and has run the same con six times before, each time scamming her "boyfriend" out of thousands of dollars. She is a wanted criminal on the run. You are now counted among the multitude who have been made victim of a lonely hearts scam.

HOW TO SPOT THE SCAM

When you're emotionally involved with someone, it's difficult to look upon requests for money objectively. But that's exactly what you must do. Especially when the request comes early in the relationship; that's almost a sure sign that a scam is approaching. Another indication is your paramour's reluctance to tell you much about her background. Meaning she's got something to hide.

HOW TO PREVENT THE SCAM

- Anytime you search for your next sweetie through lonely hearts clubs or ads, your chances of finding a financial predator are fairly high.
- Your chances of discovering somebody genuinely interested in you and not your money are enhanced if you look for your partner-to-be in your church (or synagogue or mosque), local senior center, or among friends and acquaintances.
- When you meet somebody you don't know, your first task (*before* you get involved) should be to find out everything you can about him or her prior to committing yourself emotionally. It's easier to break off a budding relationship than one that has progressed to the stage where you've lost your heart.
- Don't hand out your hard-earned dollars until you're damn good and sure it's going where your lover says it's going. What you should have done in the example described above is talk to the sister and verify the forthcoming surgery with the Mexican hospital.

Lotteries and Sweepstakes

THE SCAM

You're a stay-at-home senior who receives a letter in the mail: "Congratulations! You are a winner! You have been selected as one of the finalists in the Monte Carlo Sweepstakes. You may soon receive a certified cashier's check for $10,000 tax-free U.S. dollars. All you need to do is send a money order for $10.00 to process your entry. Our statistical experts have calculated your chances of winning at one in four. That's right, one in four. Send your $10.00 money order today." The letter can come from almost anywhere in the world, but most frequently it will arrive from Canada, Australia, or Europe.

Throwing money at lotteries and sweepstakes is a loser's game, designed to part otherwise sensible seniors from their hard-earned dollars. Frequently, those who play may be breaking the law.

Of course, this is an outright and contemptible scam. You will *never* receive any money. Literally millions of these letters find their way to the United States, and you better believe that many recipients are sending in their ten-dollar money orders because the scam continues unabated. The scammers are counting on the small entry fee to entice you.

HOW TO SPOT THE SCAM

What most seniors don't realize is that lottery solicitations such as these violate U.S. law, which prohibits the cross-border sale or purchase of lottery tickets by phone or mail. The offer, therefore, is bogus. You'll never see any prize money because there wasn't any prize money to begin with.

HOW TO PREVENT THE SCAM

- It's not only illegal for individuals or organizations to solicit your money in a foreign lottery or sweepstakes, it's also illegal for you to play. So if you receive a solicitation through the mail, over the telephone, or by e-mail over the Internet and you respond, you're violating federal law.
- If you purchase one foreign lottery or sweepstakes ticket, expect many more bogus offers to arrive. They'll virtually flood your mailbox. You are now considered a mark by the many frauds operating so-called lotteries and sweepstakes, and they'll go after your money like starving wolves after hobbled rabbits.
- If you're foolish enough to respond by credit card, your credit card number will be used to purchase goods for the benefit of the lottery scam artists.

- According to the Federal Trade Commission, the best way to handle the scam is to ignore all mail and phone solicitations for foreign lotteries or sweepstakes.

ALSO SEE: *"Prizes" (page 165).*

Prizes

THE SCAM

You're notified by mail that you've won a free Rolex watch worth in the neighborhood of $5,000. You call the toll-free telephone number shown in the letter. A salesman congratulates you and says to collect your Rolex, you will need to pay state tax on the item as well as shipping and handling charges. The total comes to $229.99, payable by credit card or money order. You're ecstatic; you've always wanted a Rolex but have never been able to afford one; this is your chance. You eagerly send in your money order. Five weeks later your prize arrives in the mail. It's a cheap imitation of a Rolex that you can buy from any street hawker in any large city for thirty bucks. You've been taken.

You've heard this before: you get what you pay for. Nobody is going to sell you a diamond necklace for $99.99. You'll get fake costume jewelry that will fall apart in three months—if you receive anything at all.

HOW TO SPOT THE SCAM

I'm sure you've heard this a thousand times before: *Little in this world comes without a price*. That's your key to spotting the scam. Yet literally thousands of seniors are scammed every year by phony offers such as the Rolex watch. Regardless of the scam—a free watch, a free car, a free vacation—enough fall for it to keep the scammers in business. All you need to do to claim your prize, they tell you, is send them the state tax. If you're foolish enough to send them anything (and I know you're not), you won't receive your prize anyway. Hey, you didn't really believe they were going to give you a free new car, did you?

HOW TO PREVENT THE SCAM

- If you've never heard of the company giving away the merchandise, that's your first indication of a scam. But beware: Some of these clever scammers disguise their names so they sound like established companies. For example, you might receive a letter in which a prize is offered from Consumer Union, which is not the same organization as Consumers Union (the publisher whose national magazine is *Consumer Reports*), but it sure looks the same, doesn't it? Major companies or organizations such as Consumers Union do give away prizes, but the piece of paper you're holding in your hand is a lead-in to a scam.
- If you're unsure about the legitimacy of the company offering the prize, contact the Better Business Bureau or your state's consumer affairs office. Even better, call consumer advocate Clark Howard's office in Atlanta, from 1:00 p.m. to 4:00 p.m.

EST, Monday through Friday at 1-404-872-0750 or toll-free 1-877-87-CLARK (only for those out of the Atlanta area). His investigative reporters will let you know if you're dealing with a legitimate company or a fraud.

- As an alternative, call your local TV station and ask to speak with its investigative consumer reporter. Her files often contain specific information about scammers.

ALSO SEE: "Lotteries and Sweepstakes" (page 162).

Event Tickets

THE SCAM

You're a senior couple who attends annual religious events around the country. Every year you try to visit different locales and meet new people of your faith. You've enjoyed this annual pilgrimage and look forward to it every year.

In a religious magazine you subscribe to, a promotional company has advertised an evangelical revival to be held in Birmingham, Alabama. It's the kind of annual event you want to attend. You call the toll-free number and sign up for two tickets at $180 each. It's a lot of money, $360, but from what you've read in the magazine, the event appears to be well worth it.

You fly to Birmingham, rent a car, and spend the night at a local motel. The next morning you drive to the site of the revival

> Event ticket scams are exploding, even for religious events. You can protect yourself by contacting the event organizers and checking on the price of tickets before you purchase them from a promoter.

and are dismayed to see that regular ticket prices are $60 and many seats are available. You've been scalped and scammed.

HOW TO SPOT THE SCAM

It's especially dismaying to be scammed by an organization promoting religious events. You would think scammers would have the decency to exempt anything to do with the church from their detestable undertakings. But they don't.

It's especially difficult because event-ticket fraud comes in many flavors: phony online auctions, used tickets, lost or stolen tickets, counterfeit tickets (so good you can't tell them from the originals), and tickets for events that don't exist.

Short answer: It's hard to spot the scam, but you can heighten your chances of preventing it by following the advice described below.

HOW TO PREVENT THE SCAM

- If you purchase an event ticket as part of a package that includes air transportation, the package falls under the consumer protection rules of the U.S. Department of Transportation (DOT). This includes sporting, social, religious, educational, cultural, political, or other events of a special nature and limited duration for which admission to the event is advertised as part of the tour. This assures some degree of protection against fraud because scammers risk violating federal and not just state law, a fact that may keep them out of the arena. (DOT protection doesn't include event tickets purchased separately from air tickets. You're on your own there.)

- But don't rely solely on the government's umbrella; oftentimes it springs leaks. If you harbor doubts about the authenticity of the tickets, or you're unfamiliar with the organization peddling the tickets, check for yourself by contacting the event's organizers to determine actual ticket prices (as well as that the event is actually taking place) before you hand over money to the event promoter.

- Once you have the tickets in hand, call the event organizer and check the ticket serial number to assure you don't have a counterfeit. If you've been conned for the price of the ticket, at least you can save yourself the airfare and motel costs.

- If you're scammed, you still may have recourse by reporting the scam to the DOT, Aviation Consumer Protection Division in Washington by calling 1-202-366-2220. The DOT may help you recover your costs.

Travel and Vacations

THE SCAM

You're a widow whose husband died recently, and the past six months have been stressful, to say the least. You need to get away. Coincidentally, the postman delivers a letter addressed to you personally, including the salutation of the letter,[42] informing you that you've won seven days at a luxury hotel on the Florida coast. Since it's winter and you're in upstate Pennsylvania (brrr, it's cold), you decide to take the trip.

> **D**eal with reputable travel agents and known hotel chains for travel and vacation plans. Don't fall for unsolicited promotions that sound too good to be true. Get plans in writing.

You fly down to Florida and rent a car and show up at the luxury hotel, only to be told that accommodations for the free rooms are filled up and you may be asked to stay at a fleabag mo-

---

[42]Don't be fooled by your name appearing in the salutation. This isn't a personal letter. You're on a database of thousands, and the software the soliciting company uses spits out dozens of those same form letters every minute.

tel five miles away. You balk, and the hotel's salesperson tells you the situation can be corrected if you decide to upgrade your reservation. You reluctantly agree and pay the difference, which amounts to more than the reasonable cost of a luxury hotel room alone, but you're in no position to argue. You've been scammed. The words "bait and switch" should come to mind, because that's exactly what happened to you.

HOW TO SPOT THE SCAM

The National Association of Attorneys General states that travel scams cost consumers $12 billion annually. In a recent sting called Operation Trip Trap, for example, the Federal Trade Commission charged twenty-five travel promoters with cheating consumers. Words in travel ads like "free trips," "free luxury hotels," and "free cruises" should alert you. In this world nobody is giving anything away for free, and you should know better. "Free" is a word that could very well mean "expensive" when found in a travel ad.

HOW TO PREVENT THE SCAM

There are a few principles to help you avoid buying into the wrong time-share or taking the wrong trip or vacation:

- When a salesperson pressures you to buy a vacation package, be wary; if it's too good to be true, it's probably a scam. Keep this principle foremost in your mind when evaluating travel plans.
- A travel scam can come at you (like any other scam) via mail, phone, e-mail, or fax. Be especially careful when the words "You have been selected to receive . . ." are printed on the

envelope. That's the typical lead-in for a phony pitch resulting in a bait-and-switch scam.

- Ask friends if they've had any experiences with the travel company soliciting your business. Then go online and use a search engine like Google or Yahoo! to see what complaints have been registered against the travel company. You can discover all kinds of dirt online about a company that would be difficult to find elsewhere.

- Get your vacation trip details nailed down in writing, particularly cancellation charges, refund policy (an emergency may force you to cancel), and the tab for taxes and services. Find out what restrictions apply, if any.

- As an added precaution, pay by credit card. Then if the travel plans or vacation do not turn out as advertised, you have the right to dispute the charges with your credit card company. And never surrender your credit card number until you're ready to sign.

- If you're interested in a charter flight, you should check the operator's legitimacy because it could be a scam that will bilk you for thousands of dollars. Don't take the chance. Using the charter operator's name and address, check its registration with the U.S. Department of Transportation (DOT), Aviation Consumer Protection Division in Washington DC by calling 1-202-366-2220. Charter packages cannot be sold until DOT approves the filing. So ask if the operator filed a charter flight from the planned departure city to the planned location. If not, you're onto a probable scam.

Shopping

The great American pastime. I don't have any scientific data to support me, but I'm willing to bet that shopping, either at home or at the mall and elsewhere, takes 10–15 percent of a senior's waking hours. I know for both my wife and myself, that percentage is not out of line. Actually, it's kind of low.

The shopping arena—a mall, a store, online, at home—is replete with scams. Whether it's a hotshot salesman selling vacuum cleaners door-to-door or a cashier taking your money at K-Mart, the opportunities for scams abound. This section describes some of the more typical shopping scams and shows how to combat them.

Door-to-Door Salesmen

THE SCAM

You're an eighty-year-old woman sitting at home watching *Oprah*. About 5:00 p.m. you hear a knock at the front door. You open it and standing in front of you is a freckle-faced young man of college age holding a vacuum cleaner. The kid has the "boy next door" looks that disarm people. It does your heart good to see such a wholesome-appearing young man. He tells you he's answering your request to have the carpets in your home cleaned free.

> If you allow door-to-door salesmen on unsolicited calls to enter your home, you're going to experience high-pressure tactics designed to wear you down and make you sign on the dotted line.

You dimly recall sending in a self-addressed postcard in response to an ad in a magazine. Well, what do you have to lose? You let him in and he starts his sales pitch, first by cleaning the carpets as promised, then by pressuring you to buy the vacuum cleaner for an outrageous sum of $1,400.

You balk, but the salesman is relentless. He wears you down. You're a widow, all alone in this world, and the salesman is cute and polite and he's company. By 7:00 p.m. you've signed a contract to purchase his product. A product you can't afford, considering you're living pretty much on Social Security and a tiny pension.

HOW TO SPOT THE SCAM

This one's easy: the moment you opened your front door and saw a stranger standing at your doorstep holding the vacuum cleaner in his hands, your troubles began. It escalated when he said he was going to clean your carpets for free. You should have remembered the old Italian proverb: "To trust is good. Not to trust is better." You let down your guard.

The scam as described above is one that's been reported about Kirby vacuum cleaners in http://www.consumeraffairs.com, http://www.ripoffreport.com, and http://www.clarkhoward.com. These Web sites, particularly the first two, describe several instances of complaints directed against Kirby, as well as legal steps state consumer affairs offices have taken to stop Kirby's alleged deceptive practices. They are cautionary tales that will alert you to all door-to-door scams, not just vacuum cleaners.

HOW TO PREVENT THE SCAM

Right off the bat you have the option to keep a pushy salesman from entering your home. If he tries to bull his way in, call 911 immediately and ask for the police.

Beyond that, the Better Business Bureau suggests the following steps *before you sign a contract or buy the product or service offered from any door-to-door salesman:*

- First, and most important, get a peephole so you can see who is at your front door. This first line of defense allows you the opportunity to visually screen a stranger.

- If you have any doubts about the salesman's authenticity, do not allow him entrance. Instead, get the name and address of the company that person allegedly represents. Let him shout it out through the door without opening it. After he leaves, call the company he represents to validate his presence, then call the Better Business Bureau to see if the company has had many complaints filed against it. If you're interested in the product, believe me, the salesman will beat a hasty path to your doorstep for a return visit.

- Assuming you have allowed him entrance and listened to his sales pitch and shown interest, don't sign on the dotted line. Legitimate companies will allow you time to think about the offer. Don't fall prey to high-pressure huckster tactics such as "This is the only chance you have," or "By tomorrow the offer is withdrawn." That's pure hogwash.

- If the service involves work around your home, verify that the contractor is properly licensed, bonded, and insured.

- If you need an expensive home repair, be especially cautious of offers that sound too good to be true. Obtain bids from several companies. Don't always go for the lowest bid—you'll get exactly what you pay for.

- Get all details of the offer for the product or service in writing and carefully review them. Make sure you understand everything in the contract. Any verbal promises should be written into the contract to prevent later misunderstandings.

- Make sure the salesperson has provided you with the proper "notice of cancellation" form as required under the FTC's Cooling-Off Rule[43] for contracts signed in the home.
- If you're satisfied with the company's reputation, and you decide to hire it or buy its product, pay with a credit card. By law (the Fair Credit Reporting Act) you'll have sixty days to dispute the charge if the goods or services were not as promised. Never pay in cash.

ALSO SEE: "*Medical Breakthroughs*" (*page 74*); "*Home Repair*" (*page 152*).

---

[43]A federal law requiring any company selling you a product or service in your home to refund your money within seventy-two hours if you so desire. Exceptions include repairs and maintenance made to your home, among others. Contact the BBB for additional details.

Gift Cards

THE SCAM

My wife, a senior of seventy years, loves to receive gift cards for Christmas and her birthday. The cards give her the option of buying whatever she wants, whenever she wants. She considers mall gift cards the best of all; they allow her to buy from any store in the mall, and there are literally dozens. It's a shopper's paradise.

Unfortunately, she often takes as long as a year to use the cards. Recently this developed into a problem. Her

> Before you buy gift cards from a store or mall for Grandma or Grandpa, make sure they don't lose value over time, as many of them do. People often hold on to gift cards for long periods before using them.

granddaughter purchased a $100 mall gift card as a birthday present that Grandma didn't use for eleven months. Imagine her shock when she went to spend the card and found that the $100 card was now worth only $73. Apparently the mall had a policy of charging $3 a month against the gift card beginning with the third month after the card was purchased. So by the time Grandma used the card, she had lost $27.

All right, you don't have to tell me: this is a small scam. But, damn it, it's a scam anyway and a stupid one at that. One that gave Grandma an unpleasant surprise. At seventy you don't need any more unpleasant surprises over and above what life already has in store for you.

HOW TO SPOT THE SCAM

You can't unless you check ahead of time and uncover the store or mall's gift card lapse policy. You can bet these scoundrels aren't advertising gift card shrinkage. From what I've been told by other shoppers, some stores even have policies that cancel the card if it hasn't been used in a year, and do not refund any portion of the money. You really need to check before buying a card for Grandma.

HOW TO PREVENT THE SCAM

Don't buy gift cards from any store or mall avaricious enough to charge any amount of money for not using its cards. And frankly, after my wife had this unpleasant experience, I took my shopping elsewhere. You can, too. Nothing speaks louder than loss of business to a store or mall.

Money-Back Guarantee

THE SCAM

Four months ago you bought a large top-freezer refrigerator from Schmovey Brothers,[44] a new appliance store in your neighborhood, for $450. This was a very good price considering the many features of the refrigerator. The salesman went out of his way to assure you that should anything go wrong with the refriger-

> The best way to assure a money-back guarantee is to get it in writing from reputable stores that have been around for a few years. Guarantees from fly-by-night stores are potentially worthless.

ator, the store would either replace it for free or give you your money back.

When you opened the refrigerator, this morning, you found everything in it defrosted, the second time this has happened. You call customer service at Schmovey. A crabby lady says you're beyond the store's warranty period of three months, and sorry, no

[44]A fictitious name.

exchange, no money back. Your only recourse is to go through the manufacturer for repair or reimbursement.

Unfortunately, you decided to buy an off-brand refrigerator made by a company in Eastern Europe to save two hundred bucks, and now you're stuck with a piece of junk. You spend three hundred dollars to repair it. Between what you paid for the refrigerator and what you spent to repair it, you could have purchased a top-of-the-line American model.

Three months later you read in the paper that Schmovey Brothers has gone out of business. You wonder how many customers like yourself were ripped off.

HOW TO SPOT THE SCAM

Two sure clues of money-back guarantees that probably won't materialize are off-brand merchandise sold through a local single-store merchant who hasn't been in business for any length of time. I once made the mistake of buying a recliner with a money-back guarantee from a questionable furniture retailer to save a few bucks. My wife and I were diverted by a charming saleslady who, like all successful salespeople, managed to connect with us emotionally so that we trusted her. It blindsided us to the inferior quality of the recliner—which predictably fell apart after a few months of use. I had to take the storeowner to small claims court to get my money back. What a hassle!

HOW TO PREVENT THE SCAM

Money-back guarantees are common among scammers peddling inferior products or services. True, some reliable businesses offer money-back guarantees, but you still have to be on guard. The guidelines for assuring a genuine money-back guarantee are:

- Get it in writing. Legitimate businesses will automatically display their money-back guarantees either on the sales slip or on separate documents that accompany the merchandise or service.
- Try to deal with recognized stores such as Wal-Mart and Home Depot or a local merchant who has been in business for many years. Stores that have a national presence (or local merchants in business for many years) have defined return policies and are easier to deal with than local merchants who do not.
- Sure, most local merchants are honest; but unless you have dealt with them before, or have heard good things about them from other customers, be cautious.
- Regardless of the merchant, make sure you fully understand under what conditions the money-back guarantee applies.

Rent to Own

THE SCAM

You're a widowed senior whose husband suffered from a debilitating illness for many years, such that the care for his illness exceeded Medicare boundaries and you were forced to eat up your savings to keep him alive. You're now alone in this world with nobody to turn to because you never had any brothers or sisters, and your two kids live 3,000 miles away.

Rent to own is the most expensive way to acquire furniture and appliances. For the rental price, you can buy two or three of the items at stores like Sears, Best Buy, or Circuit City.

Your TV just went out and you want to buy a new one, but you can't afford it. A rent-to-own store recently ran an ad in your local newspaper that caught your attention. Its six-inch display loudly proclaimed that for twelve bucks a week, you could rent a nineteen-inch TV and apply the rental payments toward eventual ownership of the set.

You decide that although the $12 a week stretches your

limited budget, you'll go ahead with the rental because TV is your only source of distraction that keeps you from mulling endlessly over the death of your husband. You sign the rental-buy agreement.

What you don't know is that a $200 rent-to-own TV is going to cost you more than a $1,000 over the life of the loan agreement. You could have gone to Best Buy or Circuit City or Sears and bought four or five TVs for the same money your one rent-to-own TV will cost you.

HOW TO SPOT THE SCAM

The State Public Interest Research Groups (http://www.pirg.org), a state and national group that speaks for the public against special interest groups, said this: "Rent-to-own stores charge an average effective annual percentage rate (APR) of 100 percent, although APRs are not disclosed." The organization also discovered that rent-to-own stores charge fees ranging from 16 percent to 275 percent for televisions and refrigerators, two of their more popular items.

The concept driving the rent-to-own business is that many consumers don't give any thought to how much they're paying over time; they're more interested in how many dollars they have to shell out every week.

This is really all you need to know about rent to own: it's cheaper to take out a loan from a bank to buy a TV than it is to rent to own.

HOW TO PREVENT THE SCAM

- If you need to rent an item, such as a dining room set for a month, rent to own is feasible. But if your intent is to keep the dining room set (or any other goods) for a longer period of time, get a loan and buy the set outright.

- If you do decide to rent to own, find out what the interest rate truly is. Before you sign the contract, take it to your banker. She'll gladly let you know what you're truly paying. It will be an eye opener.

Shopping Online

THE SCAM

You've been shopping online now for about six months and truly enjoy the convenience of both ordering and paying online. You routinely shop on eBay, Amazon, Yahoo! Shopping, and other Web sites for a variety of merchandise. You pay for your purchases at these Web sites with major credit cards or through eBay's PayPal.

> **B**uy only from established vendors such as eBay, Amazon, or the online operations of large national stores like Sears and Wal-Mart. Use the buying systems and protections they offer.

But recently, a new third-party seller on one of the shopping Web sites has enticed you to pay him directly, outside of normal buying channels, by offering a 10 percent discount. Obviously, he's attempting to avoid paying sales fees to the shopping Web site. Or so you think. What he's really doing is stealing your credit card number. If you agree and go ahead with the transaction, he will sell your credit card number along with dozens of others to a gang of thieves in major cities across the country, who will then quickly run up charges before you and other victims have a chance to discover the scam. He then disappears (only to reappear again on another shopping Web site under another name). You're the casualty of a hit-and-run merchant who really isn't a merchant at all, just a scammer.

HOW TO SPOT THE SCAM

The key signal is the so-called merchant's request to do business outside of the established business system of eBay, Yahoo! Shopping, Amazon, or other established shopping Web sites.

If you had thought about it for a moment, you would have concluded that the 10 percent discount he offered you would exceed the sales fee the shopping Web site charges him.

HOW TO PREVENT THE SCAM

The shopping Web sites offer this advice:

- Make your payments for merchandise through established business systems, and only at the shopping Web sites. Don't allow a merchant to talk you into paying with a credit card elsewhere. Each of the Web sites offer buyer's protections to prevent you from being defrauded, but only if you use their systems.
- Limit your purchases of merchandise from a new seller even on established shopping Web sites until he's established a track record. Each of the sites displays a merchant's record

that exposes problems he's had with price, delivery, and quality. But that reputation takes time to build.

- Report any attempts of sellers who ask that you purchase outside of the system to the shopping Web site administrators.

ALSO SEE: "*Bogus Web Sites*" *(page 102).*

Scanner Errors

THE SCAM

At checkout the electronic scanner doesn't ring up the correct price of a discounted item. The sneakers you thought were on sale at $29.99 show $34.99 on the green electronic display. Unless you're paying attention, you may lose that five bucks. It goes from your cash-starved pocket into the coffers of a company making tens or hundreds of million of dollars in profits every year. Guess who needs that five bucks more.

Studies have shown that electronic scanners at all stores, including the large national chains, are error prone, with more than one-half exceeding federally accepted standards.

What's that, you say? Scanner mistakes are rare, the exception that happens once in a blue moon? Well, think again. It's an everyday occurrence. In one study conducted by the Chicago Consumer Services Commissioner, investigators reported a whopping 58 percent of Chicago stores overcharge their customers at checkout. For example, seventy-two Walgreens stores in the Chicago area overcharged their customers for a variety of items. Radio Shack rang up $59.99 for a two-way radio advertised for $39.99, and Office Depot rang-up $33.98 for a surge strip advertised at $16.99.[45]

I conducted my own search online. I typed in "checkout scanner errors" in the Yahoo! search engine and came up with 121,000 hits (whew!). After scrolling through a small portion of the list, I found companies accused of overcharging at checkout (mostly through error) that reads like a retail Fortune 500: Sears, Kroger, Walgreens, Staples, K-Mart, Office Depot. The list goes on and on.

For more examples of checkout scams, go online and experiment as I did, or check The Ripoff Report (http://www.ripoffreport.com) or the Better Business Bureau (http://www.bbb.org).

HOW TO SPOT THE SCAM

The best way, other than through direct observation while you're standing at the checkout and observing every entry on the electronic cash register, is to ask friends and neighbors about their experiences with different retailers. Oftentimes, TV programs or newspaper reports will describe studies that reveal the truly appalling rate of overcharging and will name names. Forewarned is forearmed.

---

[45]From an online article "Have You Checked Your Receipts Lately?" by Jon Van Vlak, http://www.recordonline.com, May 18, 2003.

HOW TO PREVENT THE SCAM

Here's the problem: as we grow older, we tend to become distracted easily; that's an inescapable fact of aging. So the best remedy is in two parts:

- Keep your eyes glued to the register as the cashier is scanning your items. Don't chat with her, a distraction. You'll catch mistakes there.
- As soon as you're through the line, check every item on your itemized receipt. Take your time. And don't be embarrassed to return to the cashier, receipt in hand, to point out the mistake and the money owed you.

ALSO SEE: "Overcharging at Mom-and-Pop Stores" (page 194).

Overcharging at Mom-and-Pop Stores

THE SCAM

Overcharging is more common than you realize. Here's how it works: You're standing on line at Susie's, a locally owned mom-and-pop discount store. Come your turn, Susie herself rings up your purchases while chatting with you and distracting your attention. A slip of Susie's finger

> **D**eliberately overcharging is more prevalent in mom-and-pop stores than in large national chains that have more foolproof cash register systems.

and the form-fitting T-shirt you like for $11.99 rings up as $12.99. Since you've purchased about a dozen items, and you're more than likely in a hurry, all you do is give your receipt a cursory glance. The difference of one dollar isn't glaring and Susie has successfully overcharged you a buck. Not much, but if you allow it to happen over the course of a year, mistakes at the cash register add up.

HOW TO SPOT THE SCAM

Wonder just how much Susie takes home from this little scam every year? Let's assume she targets only customers who are buying several items (which includes most customers), and she makes a little "mistake" of overcharging a dollar, say every couple of hours. That's $4 a day (assuming an eight-hour shift) or $20 a week, totaling about $1,000 a year. Not bad for a few little "mistakes."

Now suppose Susie's husband Rick and daughter Marge are working the other two cash registers. That thousand bucks now becomes three thousand annually, all of it tax free. And at your expense and other customers like you. There's nobody who oversees the owners, so they get away with the overcharging. But only if you as the customer allow it.

If you keep alert and don't gab with Susie while she's ringing up your items, chances are you'll catch her slip of the finger. More than likely, if she's aware you're watching, she'll probably not scam you, just wait for the next victim in line.

HOW TO PREVENT THE SCAM

- Don't let Susie distract you so much that you don't check your itemized receipt. Do it before you leave the store.
- When you discover an "error," show the itemized receipt to Susie. Let her know that you caught her mistake. Let her know by the tone of your voice that you're on to her scam. Chances are she'll never overcharge you again.
- If Susie still tries to overcharge you, then the woman's greed is overcoming her judgment. Don't shop there again.

ALSO SEE: "Scanner Errors" (page 191).

Telephone

Let's face it: we need the telephone to survive in today's society.
It's such an integrated part of our daily lives, we'd regress a hundred years without its constant and reasonably cheap availability.
Yet the telephone can be an enormous headache if we let its problems overwhelm us. The topics in this section show you how to
manage the most common scams associated with this most vital
communications tool.

Phone Bill

THE SCAM

You open your phone bill and you're surprised to see charges for services you never ordered. There's call waiting, voice mail, and paging. These extras add up to a bundle. You're outraged and you call the phone company. You're told that you ordered the extra services. You vaguely recall taking a survey from a representative of the phone company and answering "yes" to a few questions about call waiting, voice mail, and paging. But you never intended to buy those services. The phone company obligingly cancels them. Glad you paid attention to your bill?

Cramming and slamming (two words that spell higher bills for customers), once on the wane, are returning as the communications industry undergoes rapid transformation. Pay attention to your bills.

HOW TO SPOT THE SCAM

Telephone scams nowadays come in two basic flavors: cramming and slamming. Two unpleasant words that are similarly unpleasant when you have to pay the bill.

Cramming is when your phone company loads you up with all manner of services you never asked for in the first place. Slamming is when another phone company switches your service to their company without telling you. It happens more frequently with long distance service, but it's not unheard of for local service.

Both cramming and slamming, each considered a diminished problem, are on the rise again as the telecommunications industry undergoes rapid transformation. Companies that didn't exist seven or eight years ago, such as Verizon, now dominate the industry, and AT&T is no more the powerhouse it once was. Wireless is growing exponentially. Everything's changing.

If you've been slammed, you have the right under federal law to ask for reinstatement with your original phone company. If you've been crammed, you have every right to ask the phone company for reimbursement. But you may have to prove your case.

As it stands, the only way to spot cramming and slamming is when they happen. Preventive measures are best. Check your monthly statement carefully.

HOW TO PREVENT THE SCAM

- To prevent cramming, ask your phone company for a service called bill blocking. That's how you prevent charges for extra services appearing on your phone bill without your prior agreement.

- To prevent slamming ask your phone company for what's called a pick freeze, which requires your written approval to switch your phone company.
- If you feel you've been crammed or slammed (sounds vaguely obscene, doesn't it?), contact the Federal Communications Commission at 1-888-225-5322, or go online to http://www. fcc.gov. Your state public utility commission may also be able to help.

Do-Not-Call Registry

THE SCAM

Think you're not vulnerable because the federal government passed a law forbidding telemarketing calls? Think again. Unless you registered with the Federal Trade Commission's (FTC's) Do-Not-Call Registry, you're open season.[46] The fact is, telemarketers abound, and they particularly love getting seniors on the line because they perceive old folks like you and me as easy marks.

> If you're still getting frequent calls from telemarketers, chances are you're not listed in the Federal Trade Commission's Do-Not-Call Registry. A toll-free call will change that.

---

[46]There are exceptions: telephone calls from or on behalf of political organizations, charities, and telephone surveyors. Organizations with which you have an established business relationship can call you up to eighteen months after your last purchase even if your number is on the national Do-Not-Call Registry. And companies to which you've made an inquiry or submitted an application can call you for three months.

HOW TO SPOT THE SCAM

You're getting frequent telephone calls from telemarketers (by landline, and increasingly, cell phone), and the calls come any time during the day or evening hours. No matter what you do—hang up, tell them to go away, slam down the phone—the calls continue. What can you do?

HOW TO PREVENT THE SCAM

- Register your telephone number with the national Do-Not-Call Registry, toll-free at 1-888-382-1222 (TTY 1-866-290-4236) or register online at http://www .donotcall.gov. Registration is free and lasts five years, at which time you will need to renew. Within three months after your initial registration, the number of annoying telephone calls you receive should drop to tolerable levels.
- When organizations call that are permitted exceptions to the FTC's telemarketing rule, tell them politely to put you on their Do-Not-Call list. By law, they are obligated not to call again.

Incidentally, do not for a moment believe that breaking the Do-Not-Call law is the sole province of small companies and fly-by-night telemarketing firms. Larger, more recognizable names are sometimes involved. For example, New York State's Attorney General Eliot Spitzer reached a settlement with The Great Atlantic & Pacific Tea Company (A&P) to stop the company from calling sweepstakes entrants whose telephone numbers are on the Do-Not-Call Registry.[47]

ALSO SEE: "Telemarketing Sales" (page 204).

---

[47]Online article "A&P Tricked Consumers into Waiving Their Do Not Call Rights," Consumer Affairs May 3, 2005, http://www.consumeraffairs.com/news04/2005/aandp.html.

Telemarketing Sales

THE SCAM

You're still not home free. The woods are full of telemarketers who are willing to break the law in "hit and run" telemarketing schemes, where they make a fast buck, then shut down their boiler room (a bank of telephones staffed by fast-talking telemarketers), move to another location, and start again.

> Seniors are desired targets for telemarketers, who view us as patsies. Follow the advice in this article and I can assure you that bothersome telemarketers will shun your telephone number.

How they *love* to prey on seniors, especially older seniors, those defenseless folks in their eighties whose intellectual capacities they perceive as diminished by time.

These unconscionable frauds make their calls, usually later in the evening when folks are tired and not as fast on their feet as they might have been earlier in the day.[48] They pitch schemes

---

[48]It's illegal for telemarketers to call past 9:00 p.m., but this doesn't seem to deter some.

ranging from investments to charities, using glib spiels to convince seniors to part with their hard-earned money. They routinely use intimidation bordering on actual threats to extort money. These frauds claim that if you don't buy *immediately*—say a thousand shares of some phony penny stock—some bully will show up on your doorstep the following morning and make you see the light. Of course, they're counting on scaring the wits out of some frightened old widow or widower. And too often their deceptions work.

Fraud.com (http://www.fraud.com) estimates that 14,000 unlawful telemarketing boiler rooms scam U.S. citizens to the tune of $40 billion annually. Surveys by AARP[49] reveal that half or more of telemarketing scam victims are age fifty or older.

HOW TO SPOT THE SCAM

Spotting the scam is as direct as picking up your phone when it rings to hear some beguiling pitchman try to weasel you out of your money.

Specifically, telemarketers are *forbidden* by federal law to:

- Call before 8:00 a.m. or after 9:00 p.m.
- Misrepresent themselves or what they're soliciting.
- Harass you if you request they not call again.

Specifically, telemarketers are *required* by federal law to:

- Tell you exactly what they're soliciting.
- Inform you of the selling company's name.

[49]Formerly the American Association of Retired Persons.

- Tell you up front that this is a sales call.
- Disclose the exact cost and terms of what they're selling, including provisions for refunds and cancellations.

HOW TO PREVENT THE SCAM

- Here's what I like to do, recognizing that time is money to a telemarketer and nothing interferes with her earning ability more than spending excessive time on any single call: Immediately after answering the phone, I ask her to kindly wait for a moment, then I gently lay the phone down on the table, the line still open. And I don't pick up the phone again until I hear the dial tone. After a short wait, the telemarketer making the call will grow fidgety and restless knowing that time's a wasting. She'll call out a few loud "hellos." When she doesn't hear anything in return, she'll grow impatient and shortly afterward hang up, then tell her associates to avoid calling my line and wasting their time.
- Sure, if you want to report her to the Do-Not-Call Registry, that's fine. But it might take months before the telemarketing operation is fined, if ever (pardon my cynicism). Take the action I recommend and pretty soon your unwanted telemarketing sales calls will dry up.

ALSO SEE: "Do-Not-Call Registry" (page 201).

Unlisted Telephone Number

THE SCAM

You're a sophisticated senior, well aware of the identity-theft problems confronting you, and with a determination not to fall victim. A telephone company salesperson persuades you to get an unlisted telephone number, for which you pay a premium monthly fee in the belief it will afford you some protection not only from identity thieves but also from annoying telemarketers.

You're later shocked to discover that identity thieves know your name and address

> **Y**ou probably don't know this, but your unlisted telephone number is for sale on the Internet. There is a more foolproof way to avoid unwanted calls, and it won't cost you a nickel.

and unlisted telephone number and have used that information to fool a bank clerk into giving them your checking account number.

How in the world is this possible, you ask yourself, since your telephone number is unlisted?

HOW TO SPOT THE SCAM

What you probably don't know is that your unlisted telephone number is for sale over the Internet. Check it out for yourself. Conduct an Internet search using these words: "unlisted telephone numbers." You'll find literally a dozen or more Web sites with unlisted telephone numbers for sale. You'll discover that your private unlisted telephone number, along with your name and address, are for sale for anywhere from $9.95 to $14.00 to anybody willing to pay the fee.

The inevitable conclusion is that unlisted numbers are no longer secure in the age of technology and the Internet.

HOW TO PREVENT THE SCAM

- Here's what several of my associates do to remain anonymous:[50] the women list their telephone numbers in the phone book under their unmarried names; the men list their names under their wives' unmarried names or as a made-up name. Mr. Jones becomes A. Smith, Mrs. Black becomes J. North in the phone book, *without an accompanying address*. The phone company shouldn't care what name you use[51] or if you don't list your address, as long as you pay the bill and there is no illegal purpose involved, and the made-up name isn't frivolous, like Peter Rabbit.

[50]Often a necessity in the age of identity theft.

[51]It shouldn't, but sometimes does. If so, talk with a phone company supervisor and convince her that your intention is not to break any law, but to simply protect yourself.

- Using a first initial instead of a name protects women from crank callers or predators, since an initial can stand for either a man or woman's name. The unmarried or made-up name is useful too, because identity thieves trying to scam you will be unable to match your name with other information they may have about you. Not listing the address makes it more difficult for identity thieves to walk away with vital information about you. It's just another defense against criminals who want to steal your personal information.

- This technique is also helpful in spotting telemarketing calls. When you pick up the phone and some disembodied voice asks to talk to whatever fake name you're listed under, it'll be immediately apparent a telemarketer is about to ply his miserable craft. Then do what I suggest in the "Telemarketing Sales" section (page 204). Set the phone down with the line open and don't put the receiver back in the cradle until you hear a dial tone. Nothing discourages telemarketers more than losing time on any single call, because time is money to these rascals.

ALSO SEE: *"Telemarketing Sales" (page 204).*

Work

Trust in God, but tie up your camel.

—ARAB PROVERB

Many seniors are of working age, not yet into retirement, or they're past retirement age but choose to work (I'm one of them). This section explores the pitfalls associated with work-related scams and describes how to avoid the more prevalent of them.

Career Marketing

THE SCAM

You're a fifty-five-year-old mid-level corporate manager, old enough to be classified a senior yet still working. Unfortunately your company is cutting back. Bottom line: you've just been laid off. What do you do? You try the traditional routes of answering job ads in the newspapers or over the Internet and sending resumes to recruiters.

After a few months with little or no response, you receive a call from a lady who identifies herself as vice president of a management company. She says your credentials are superb, and the president of her company and his staff, who have untold numbers of high-level executive contacts, would like to discuss career opportunities with you. You're elated. Finally, it appears as if you're going to be recog-

> Unemployed people pay career-marketing firms up to $20,000 to teach them job-hunting skills. Those same skills are available in any number of books for twenty-five bucks or less.

nized for your true capability and record of achievements.

You arrive for your appointment and one of the slickest salesmen you've ever met convinces you to enroll in the career marketing company's counseling program that, combined with the contacts of the company's staff, will magically open the door to opportunities you've only heretofore dreamed possible. Price tag: $8,000. The "management" company is really a career-marketing company. You buy the program and you've just washed eight grand down the drain for something you could have done yourself by going to the bookstore and buying *What Color Is Your Parachute?* or similar books that describe how to network to find jobs. Cost to you: about twenty-five bucks (or free at a public library). Sure beats shelling out eight grand, doesn't it?

HOW TO SPOT THE SCAM

Career marketing (also called career management, executive marketing, or a slew of other names formulated to allure out-of-work executives and managers) has been around for over fifty years. It started in the 1950s when a few entrepreneurial businessmen decided there was a market in unemployed managers and executives. They concocted a program that's dedicated to uncovering the so-called hidden job market, in essence a gimmick that in reality means learning how to network (building on leads from businesspeople, friends, and associates).

You can spot the approaching scam when somebody you don't know other than a recruiter calls to tell you how her company can help you locate job openings or put you in touch with executives who can. That's contrary to reality. In the job market it's incumbent upon job seekers to go knocking on doors themselves; it is truly a rare circumstance when somebody chases an unemployed manager to fill a position. That happens only when the unemployed senior has a specialized skill that's in demand.[52] And if that's the case, he or she won't be out of work for long, so why pay a career-marketing firm?

HOW TO PREVENT THE SCAM

- Whenever somebody calls and claims her company can find a job for you, it's either a recruiter (who frankly, doesn't often call unemployed managers or executives) or a telemarketer from a career-marketing company avidly pursuing access to your hard-earned cash. Hang up the phone.

- Beware of the career-marketing person who claims to be a recruiter and entices you with the prospects of choice job openings. Chances are those openings don't exist. Always ask up front if the so-called recruiter charges a fee for his work. If he says yes or dodges the question, hang up.

- Suspect any claims made by career-marketing salespeople who claim to be able put you in touch with executives of hiring companies. That's just not the real world. Assuming they sucker twenty out-of-work job candidates into their program every month (a not uncommon number) and claim to put each candidate in touch with three executives, that amounts to 720 referrals (20 candidates per month × 3 referrals each × 12 months). Their ridiculous claim kind of falls apart when exposed to daylight, doesn't it?

- If you've already been ripped off by a career-marketing firm, contact your state attorney general or consumer affairs office

[52]Or is a high-profile CEO. But such executives don't usually need to use career-marketing services.

to get your money back. You may also consider going to small claims court. This court has a history of being sympathetic to victims of career-marketing frauds.

ALSO SEE: "Recruiters" (page 219).

Franchises

THE SCAM

You've invested wisely and, although a senior, you're young enough and you want to work a few extra years in your own business. You answer an ad in the paper for an electronic security device franchise. The franchise owner, a hot-shot salesman, sells you the package. You plunk down most of your available cash and you're in business.

> **F**ew people make money in the franchise business (other than those selling franchises). The franchise business is awash with phony business opportunities run by scam artists.

Unfortunately, once you've been divested of your money, you rarely get to see the franchise owner; he's lost interest. Further investigation reveals you've got more competition than the franchise owner promised; there is no protected market territory for you. Other franchisees you've contacted are all madder than hell. They, too, feel they've been rooked. With a sinking feeling in your stomach, you realize you could have done better with your money by stashing it away in a bank certificate of deposit earning 4 percent interest.

HOW TO SPOT THE SCAM

Ask to talk with other franchise investors *before* you make any commitment. And not with just one or two; talk with several. If there's something phony about the franchise, it should surface.

Talk with competitors. Look over their operations. Check out your region ahead of time and make sure you truly do have a protected market territory.

HOW TO PREVENT THE SCAM

There are certain signs that the franchise is a scam. These are discernible before you hand over your money:

- The franchise owner promises unheard-of profits. He describes a virtual money tree. Believe me, if that were true, he wouldn't be running ads in the newspapers to get investors. They'd be flocking to him.
- He may even guarantee a base level of profits. This is a possible indication of a scam because few franchise owners are going to prop up their franchisees' operations. It could be a sign of desperation and a tip-off to the franchise owner's shaky financial situation.
- The same comment holds true for any money-back guarantee the franchise owner makes. Watch the contract wording

carefully: the money-back guarantee may be tied to procedures the franchise owner makes so stringent that you'll never be able to meet them.

ALSO SEE: *"Work-at-Home Schemes" (page 222).*

Recruiters

THE SCAM

You answer an ad run by a recruiter in the jobs section of the Sunday newspaper. Three days later you receive a call from the recruiter and an invitation to meet at her offices. You accept and show up on time dressed in your best business suit. She warmly welcomes you, then launches into a twenty-minute spiel about a job she thinks you're perfect for. She was wondering if you'd like to be considered for it.

You leap at the opportunity. You're an unemployed fifty-eight-year-old middle manager,

> While many honest recruiters ply their craft, others are cheats. You'll need to learn the difference if you expect to take advantage of their services and find meaningful employment.

and not many companies have expressed an interest in you. Most men your age who can expect to easily find new jobs are usually employed and at least at the vice-presidential level, or they possess a specialized skill that's in demand.

Just one catch, the recruiter explains: you've got to pay her commission because the hiring company refuses to do so. And if you don't get the job, you're still obligated to pay half her normal fee for the work she's going to put in on your behalf.

Ninety-nine times out of one hundred this is a scam. I recruited managers for client companies when I ran a consulting firm, and I can tell you from experience that any company refusing to pay the recruiting fee for a middle-management job or higher is probably a company you don't want to work for. The chances of a legitimate opportunity coming along under such circumstances are indeed slim. And the idea of paying a fee to an unsuccessful recruiter is utterly preposterous.

Your best option is to politely tell the recruiter where she can put her job, exit immediately, and report her to the Better Business Bureau and the consumer affairs office of your state.

HOW TO SPOT THE SCAM

Your first clue should be the telephone call from the recruiter, a come-on if there ever was one. Frankly, most legitimate recruiters are not going to go after older unemployed middle managers like yourself, not when the hopper is full of younger versions already employed, the clear preference of both recruiters and employers. Not unless you possess a specialized and hard-to-find skill needed in the marketplace. But if your skills are in demand, why should you pay a fee? It should be the other way around; you should receive a starting bonus. And regardless of your circumstances, you should never pay a fee to an unsuccessful recruiter. Period.

HOW TO PREVENT THE SCAM

Far be it from me to tell you that under no circumstances should you accept the interview offered by the recruiter. Perhaps it's the opportunity of a lifetime and for some obscure reason the hiring company refuses to pay the fee.

- By all means take the interview. If you receive an offer, ask the hiring company if it will pay the recruiting fee. Once you have an offer in hand, all the company can do is say no. After that, it's your decision.
- But my educated guess is that the recruiter is trying to take advantage of your desperation to find work and scam you. No legitimate offer will be forthcoming. Perhaps she and the human resources manager of the hiring company are in this scam together, splitting the fees from literally dozens of unemployed people like you. Don't become one of their victims.
- If you've already been ripped off by a recruiting firm, contact your state attorney general or consumer affairs office. You may also consider going to small claims court. This court is sympathetic to victims of such crimes.

ALSO SEE: "Career Marketing" (page 212).

Work-at-Home Schemes

THE SCAM

You're a retired senior with a lot of time to spare. You don't play golf and you're traveled out. You've had all the worldwide trips, cruises, and vacations in exotic climates you can handle. Now you want something to occupy your time and perhaps make a few bucks.

> Beware of work-at-home schemes that ask for money up front or that ask you to purchase materials or kits, or those that claim you can make millions by hiring other people. Most are phony.

You don't want to take the traditional senior route and drive a school bus, work as a substitute teacher, or flip hamburgers at Burger King. Nothing there appeals to you.

You've been impressed with opportunities other seniors have been capitalizing on to open online businesses, especially through Web sites such as eBay. You think this might be just the opportunity you're seeking.

You answer an Internet ad advertising a variety of online businesses, ranging from selling specialty shoes to starting your own matchmaking business.

A few days later you receive a call from a woman who identifies herself as the owner of the business whose ad you answered. She delights you with an enthusiastic sales pitch about the opportunities. The lady talks you into sending her a check for $49.95 plus $6.25 shipping and handling for a comprehensive manual that will show you step by step how to start your own online business. You dutifully send in your check for $56.20, and three weeks later you receive in the mail a puny fourteen-page typed and stapled report that looks as if it had been put together by a demented monkey. The contents live up to the appearance of the so-called manual; it contains nothing more than generalized advice you could have found for free on the Internet or in the library. You've been scammed and you're boiling mad.

HOW TO SPOT THE SCAM

It comes down to this when you're dealing with somebody you don't know, particularly somebody online: don't jump in until you've given yourself time to investigate and verify the legitimacy of the work.

HOW TO PREVENT THE SCAM

- Do some basic research. Go to your local library and ask for *The Work at Home Sourcebook* or find it online at http:// workathomesourcebook.com. You'll discover a listing of legitimate work-at-home businesses, some that are real moneymakers, most not as lucrative, but all spelled out in enough detail to give you some idea about the moneymaking potential of each. The choice is yours.

- Be wary of any work-at-home offer sent to you via e-mail. Many are either bogus or marginal in terms of what kind of money you can expect to earn. Remember, the Internet is still like the Wild West of the late 1800s. It's unregulated and dangerous if you don't take precautions. Draw your six-gun, pardner!

- Avoid get-rich-quick schemes, particularly those promising that you can become wealthy working part time. That's simply not going to happen.

- Be especially wary of any work-at-home offer that claims to advance you earnings before you start work. The offer is usually accompanied by a request to mail in a processing fee before you receive the advance. This is a blatant come-on. I guarantee the advance will fail to materialize. (C'mon, what company is going to send you money if it doesn't know anything about you?)

- And the converse of that: don't send money to the company to buy materials or kits or anything else. The purpose is to have them pay you, not you pay them. If they insist on it, tell them you'll reimburse them out of your first paycheck.

- Ask for basic information about the work-at-home offer: company history, years in business, products or services offered, amount of money most work-at-home people earn with the company. Legitimate companies will willingly send you a packet laying out the details.

- Nail down the payment specifics. Are you on salary or piecework? What are the rates? How often do you get paid? Will the company withhold money for taxes or will you assume contractor status?

- Get references. Ask others who have tried the work-at-home offer questions such as are its managers honest and reliable, what kind of money can you realistically expect to make, and the amount of work involved.
- Understand the legalities of the business. Some work-at-home offers like medical billing may require state licensing. Most counties will require you to obtain a business license for any work done at home. There may also be local zoning ordinances or subdivision covenants that prohibit or restrict work at home.
- Be wary of any work that involves data entry, stuffing envelopes, assembling kits, recruiting other people[53] or processing claims. These usually turn out to be impractical schemes or pay little for much work.

ALSO SEE: "Franchises" (page 216).

---

[53]Also called multi-level marketing (MLM). A scheme in which a salesperson geometrically expands the amount of commissions he or she earns by recruiting others to sell the same product or service. Very few people have the talent and drive to build such an organization.

Appendix A

Five Rules Seniors Should Follow to Avoid Investment Scams

How One Senior Couple Almost Lost $50,000

WHAT LED US TO THE WOLF'S DOOR

How's this for a sweet problem? My wife had a mid-six-figure investment in Series EE bonds with ten years left to maturity and a financial decision to make: should she cash in all the bonds up front or spread the cash-out over ten years? Her objective was preservation of capital.

My wife and I are in our early seventies, with enough existing savings from investments other than the savings bonds to support us comfortably until eighty. From a practical point of view, living another twenty years is not probable, but from a financial point of view, it's a necessary planning horizon. To assume we had only ten years left to live and spend the savings-bond money in that ten-year span would make us dependent on our children for support if we lived past eighty. Something neither my wife nor I were prepared to do.

THE WOLF WAS DRESSED IN A BROOKS BROTHERS SUIT

Her foray into the financial arena to solve this dilemma started promisingly enough. The branch of the financial company she visited—one of the country's largest and most prestigious—was located in a towering chrome, steel, and glass building in a modern business park, surrounded by manicured shrubs and flowers and winding walks.

Its suite of offices was equally impressive: marble hallways, heavy, solid cherry and mahogany furniture, gilt-framed oil paintings—the entire scenario devoted to creating an impression of wealth and power.

Here was a rock-solid and reputable firm that would focus on our financial needs without taking us to the cleaners. Its very size and grandeur gave her a warm and glowing feeling.

My wife's financial advisor was similarly impressive. A tall guy around forty, going to gray around the temples, and dressed in a custom-made Brooks Brothers suit. His list of financial credentials included every acronym known to mankind and then some. Kind of swept her off her feet.

RULE #1: When your assets are on the line, remember the wolf who dressed in Grandma's clothing. Damned animal almost snookered Little Red Riding Hood into becoming his latest meal. So don't be fooled by appearances.

Impressive financial advisors in impressive offices in impressive buildings in impressive office parks don't necessarily equate to impressive investment advice. If anything, they tend to cloud your judgment. The reality isn't in the surroundings; it's in the investment advice you get.

THE WOLF SHOWS HIS PEARLY WHITES

My wife's financial advisor smiled and assured her he was a "no pressure" kind of guy, and that his most important goal was to design an investment strategy my wife and I would be comfortable with. She believed him (as I would have, too) and let her guard down. They talked for an hour about our net worth and financial needs. She remembers stating clearly that, given our ages, preservation of capital was our primary goal.

Her guru told her he had somebody special he'd like her to meet, an annuities specialist, and asked if she had the time now to meet him. Not knowing what to expect, she said yes.

RULE #2: Hold onto your wallet when wolves double-team you. If they smell blood they go into a feeding frenzy. You're liable to lose a portion of every asset you own in the name of sales commissions.

What more appetizing target for investment wolves than a seventy-year-old woman? And let's face it, older people are vulnerable. Seniors are simply not as sharp as they were at thirty or forty, not as on top of things, more fearful and less prone to take risks, and more likely to make mistakes.

The double-team tactic made popular by car dealers fifty years ago is still flourishing, and not only in the automobile industry. In the typical double-team ploy, a car dealer's salesperson supposedly tries to get you, the customer, the best deal and has to fight his sales manager for a lower price (chuckle, chuckle). I'm sure most of you have been exposed to this ridiculous charade. But are sleazy double-teaming tactics appropriate for a so-called prestigious investment house, particularly when used against defenseless seniors? Unfortunately, it's widespread.

VARIABLE WHAT?

The annuities expert made his pitch. Both he and my wife's financial wizard applied pressure. She sat between them and felt as if her defenses were getting battered from both sides like a tennis ball in a sizzling match.

Simply put, they were pushing variable annuities.[54] She didn't know it at the time (and neither did I), but according to Clark Howard, arguably America's #1 consumer advocate, "the time to buy variable annuities is never."[55] Indeed, more and more gullible seniors are scammed into cashing in their life savings, even taking mortgages out on their homes, to enter the promised world of variable annuities. Financial salespeople push them because— you guessed it—most variable annuities generate hefty sales commissions. The particular variable annuity this dynamic duo was championing would have cost my wife over fifteen grand up front, not to mention a whopping 2 percent of her invested capital *every year*. Is it no wonder that variable annuities are the wet dreams of financial salespeople?

[54]See "Variable Annuities" (page 141).

[55]From the Clark Howard Show, "The Time to Buy Variable Annuities Is Never," May 18, 2005. Go to www.clarkhoward.com and type "variable annuities" in the search engine. You'll find a dozen or so other places where Clark comments on variable annuities.

RULE #3: When the first words out of your financial advisor's mouth are "variable annuity"—especially before he's had the opportunity to examine your financial needs and goals—hang up the phone or walk out of his office and find a new financial advisor. Or, if you're so inclined, drop-kick the rogue to Pittsburgh.

My wife and I would talk later with four other financial firms: two of them large and national, one small and local. The fourth was the investment arm of a large bank. With the exception of the bank, the others were obsessed with pushing variable annuities with bloated up-front sales commissions. Only the bank mentioned no-load bond mutual funds and tax-deferred government bonds. None of the others truly attempted to develop a personalized investment strategy for us based on our inviolate principle of preservation of capital.

NOW YOU SEE IT, NOW YOU DON'T

Back to my wife's very own financial guru. Both of us were curious to see his final recommended investment strategy. Even hopeful, despite the frustrations she felt from being double-teamed.

On the next visit, I joined my wife and we met with him. He whipped out a bound computerized report of forty or so pages, and proudly informed us that it contained our own personalized investment strategy, designed specifically with our goals in mind. Sure enough, our names were printed on the cover in gilt-colored letters.

The report itself was so technically obtuse as to dazzle the senses and blind us to the existence of the sizable sales commissions it was designed to generate. It was replete with technical terms only a financial insider could understand, along with fold-out graphs containing lines of different colors that zigged and zagged in every direction. Supplemented by copious footnotes, of course. Forty pages crammed with arcane financial details.

The financial whiz flipped through the pages so quickly my wife and I couldn't form opinions or ask intelligent questions. By the time he reached the last page I had a blinding headache and a knot in my stomach. My wife looked similarly upset. He pressed us for a decision.

RULE #4: Never make a decision on the spot in the presence of a financial advisor. Never. Regardless of how much pressure your financial advisor applies. If you do not remember anything else about this story, remember this.

Take the proposal home. See if your spouse makes sense of it. If you're having difficulty understanding the proposal, ask a trusted advisor such as your lawyer or CPA to explain it. How about your kids? If they're not knowledgeable about investments, perhaps they know somebody who is. Dispassionately assess whether or not the proposal meets your financial goals. *Take as much time as you need*. Ignore the daily phone calls from your financial advisor pressuring you to buy.

As my wife and I discovered later, the proposal was in opposition to our stated goal of preservation of capital. It would have had my wife switch from a fully subscribed fixed annuity, now paying out monthly, to a new variable annuity with surrender fees and a $15,000 sales commission. Moreover, the financial whiz wanted to move her from government savings bonds into mutual funds composed of 60 percent common stocks and 40 percent bonds. And he had the audacity to call that a conservative allocation of assets. A more appropriate financial strategy for her would have been 100 percent bonds. Of course, the mutual funds he proposed—you guessed it—carried substantial commissions and inflated yearly fund expenses.

THE BAD AND THE UGLY. THE REALLY UGLY.

I've saved the really ugly part for last. My wife's advisor tried every way to persuade her to cash in her savings bonds immediately rather than spread them over ten years. He claimed appreciation on savings bonds would be taxed as capital gains at a rate significantly lower than ordinary income. Of course, that was an outright lie. There is no appreciation on savings bonds other than interest earned. And interest earned on savings bonds is taxed as regular income, not capital gains. I call this deception unprincipled, possibly even unlawful.

He also claimed that as interest rates rise, the price of the bonds would fall. Seeing that interest rates were on the rise, that comment was designed to persuade my wife to sell now. But prices and interest rates for savings bonds, unlike other treasury securities and corporate bonds, are set by the government, not the market. Contrary to what he told my wife, no relationship exists between interest rates and savings-bond prices. Yet another lie in the financial guru's endless arsenal of deceit.

He had thrown so much information at my wife and I in such a short time that we became confused and disoriented, unsure of what was truth, what was not, what to do next. Not an unusual reaction for seniors up against a younger and sharper adversary (don't ever believe for one moment this person is your friend and confidant; he is not).

He pressed my wife and me for a decision and insisted on having one before we left the office. When we balked, his tone became more urgent, more demanding. He warned of dire consequences if we didn't act now. (The last refuge of a dishonest salesperson watching his sales commission slipping away.) When my wife told him that we would ask our banker son to review the proposal before making a decision, he deflated faster than a punctured balloon.

Still, I had to admit his line was seductive enough that my wife and I found ourselves willing to be convinced. These guys are nothing if not slick. After my son looked over this proposal, he told us that had we followed her financial guy's advice—cashing in the savings bonds up front and converting her existing annuity to a variable annuity—it would have cost her close to $50,000 in extra taxes and sales commissions. That's a lot of money for your average senior citizen to flush down the drain.

RULE #5: The words "buyer beware" should be stamped across the head of every senior when it comes to investments. Whatever you do, don't naively assume your financial advisor won't cross the line into duplicity to make a sale. It happened to us; it can happen to you.

Seniors are particularly vulnerable to wolves in the investment community, those waiting patiently in their fancy offices like wolves in their dens, salivating at the thought of fleecing yet another elderly financial innocent. Keep a critical attitude about you and you'll survive without losing your shirt (and pants and jacket and shoes, etc.).

Appendix B

Helpful Resources

HOW TO USE THE RESOURCES LISTED ON THE FOLLOWING PAGES

The organizations listed below are information resources. If you're having a problem with a particular scam and you want help, go to the appropriate section and contact the listed organization. Normally each organization has abundant information to help you identify scams and protect against them. If they have Web sites (most do), visiting online should be your first stop. You can contact many sources through their toll-free numbers.

You should realize that information resources on the Internet change frequently. A Web site here today may change its name or contents tomorrow, even disappear. Since the lead time from writing this book to having it published is about a year, it's entirely possible you may have trouble locating a few Web sites I recommend. In that case I suggest typing the subject you're looking for in Google (http://www.google.com) or some other search engine. Once you've learned to navigate the Internet, searching will become second nature.

I have no financial interest, financial inducement, or other tie-ins with the organizations listed below. And, with certain exceptions such as the Better Business Bureau, my personal experience is limited to an examination of their Web sites or communicating with a few people who are familiar with their services. So I am unable to endorse any specific organization or vouch for the accuracy of its claims. Use your good common sense: learn about scams from each resource, but if any want fees for their services, I suggest you check them out *carefully* before you spend your hard-earned money. My intent here is to help you get started researching on your own (not do your specific search for you), and to provide you with additional resources and ideas that will help reduce your vulnerability to scams. The rest is up to you.

COMMERCIAL RESOURCES

The organizations listed here are excellent resources that supplement this book. Each Web site listed below has a slightly different slant that will allow you to explore different aspects of scams:

http://www.consumeraffairs.com is an excellent resource exposing a wide variety of consumer fraud.

http://www.ripoffreport.com describes consumer complaints (in consumers' own words) for all types of suspect and defective goods and services, and along the way exposes the most reprehensible scams in the marketplace. You can file your own complaint at this Web site. Make your voice heard.

http://www.clarkhoward.com is the Web site of arguably America's favorite consumer reporter, and certainly its most charismatic. His Web site describes many of the more common senior scams. Call his office in Atlanta, GA, from 1:00 p.m. to 4:00 p.m. EST, Monday through Friday at 404-872-0750 or toll-free 1-877-87-CLARK (only for those outside the Atlanta area).

http://www.corp.ca.gov. The California Department of Corporations has an excellent section of its public service Web site devoted to exposing senior scams. You can also reach it toll-free at 1-866-275-2677.

http://www.fraud.com. The Web site for Fraud.com has a comprehensive list of common scams that hook vulnerable seniors.

http://www.pirg.org. The State Public Interest Research Groups speaks for public interest against special interests. Its Web site contains an excellent description of common senior scams along with preventive measures.

http://www.bbb.com. The granddaddy of all scam busters, the Better Business Bureau. A fine resource to understand scams as well as rate the performance of individual companies you're considering buying products or services from.

http://www.aarp.org. AARP's Web site. Another standard resource for seniors who want a guide to everyday senior problems and how to handle them.

http://www.consumerreports.org. The Web site of *Consumer Reports*. Subscribing to this excellent magazine—print issue or online subscription or both—makes for a comprehensive archive of valuable information. I collect the magazines and refer to them frequently. They've saved my wife and I a bundle of dollars and spared us a lot of headaches.

http://www.consumerworld.org. Consumer World is an advocacy group. Its Web site contains contact information for both government agencies and corporations that aid consumers.

GOVERNMENT RESOURCES

http://www.consumeraction.gov. The Web site of the General Services Administration's Consumer Action Handbook. This handy volume, revised yearly, is one of the best resources I've ever come across for advising consumers on a variety of common scams facing them. It is 160 pages packed with valuable information. Best of all, it's free. Order toll-free at 1-888-878-3256.

http://www.ftc.gov. The Federal Trade Commission (FTC). A prime information source for identity theft problems, credit card fraud, and related senior scams.

http://www.fcc.gov. The Federal Communications Commission (FCC). This agency handles complaints regarding telephone and telemarketing fraud, and scams related to radio, television, wire, wireless devices, satellite, and cable.

http://www.ssa.gov. The Social Security Administration (SSA). Contact its toll-free fraud line at 1-800-269-0271 if you suspect your Social Security number has been used by identity thieves.

http://sec.gov. The U.S. Securities and Exchange Commission (SEC). The agency that investigates securities fraud (remember Martha Stewart?). If you suspect you've been financially duped, this is a good place to start the complaint process.

ANTI-VIRUS SOFTWARE

There are many anti-virus software packages on the market that provide initial protection plus the opportunity to receive automatic updates, allowing you to stay protected against literally thousands of newly-discovered viruses. Three of the more commonly used software programs that offer online automatic updates are shown here:[56]

http://www.symantec.com/downloads. Symantec's Web site for its flagship Norton anti-virus software.

http://download.mcafee.com/us/upgradeCenter/datRenewal. asp. McAfee's Web site.

http://www.trendmicro.com/en/home/us/personal.htm. Trend Micro's Web site.

McAfee and Trend Micro offer free online anti-virus scans, but you shouldn't rely solely on free scans to protect you from viruses. They'll bring you up to date for that moment, but from that point onward, you're on your own. For complete protection you'll need to purchase the software to stay updated.

[56]Omit the final period when typing these Web site addresses into the Internet.

CHECK FRAUD

http://www.ckfraud.org/ckfraud.html. The National Check Fraud Center. This Web site will show you how to protect yourself against fraudulent checks. Call 1-843-571-2143 for specific requests.

CAR REPAIRS

http://nhtsa.gov. The National Highway Traffic Safety Administration maintains a file of service bulletins issued by car manufacturers. Check here to see if your car is listed. Even if the car is out of warranty, the manufacturer may pay for the repair if the problem is listed in one of its service bulletins. If you click the link "Recalls," you will find if your car has been recalled for a safety hazard (although by law the dealer or manufacturer is required to notify you by mail). Call toll-free 1-800-424-9393.

http://www.autosafety.org. The Center for Auto Safety is a one-stop source of information on service bulletins, recalls, state lemon laws, and other information about car safety and repair. Call 1-202-328-7700 or visit the Web site.

http://www.safetyforum.com. If you've bought a lemon, register it here on the message board as a warning to other buyers. Or see what other buyers' experiences have been before you buy your car. The Web site also lists tort lawyers who bring suit against car companies and automotive parts manufacturers.

http://www.auto-repair-warranty.com/service_consulting. htm. If you don't have a local advisor who can make sure you're not getting ripped off by a car repair shop, this service may be for you. Or it may give you some ideas how to search for a reputable garage locally. But remember, this is a paid service, so check it out before you buy.

For resolving disputes regarding lemons or car repairs, try these additional sources:

http://www.nada.com. The National Automobile Dealers Association. Toll-free 1-800-252-6232. For beefs with car dealers.

http://www.ase.com. The National Institute for Automotive Service Excellence. Call 1-703-669-6600. For complaints against service shops you're having trouble resolving.

http://thelemonlaw.org. The International Association of Lemon Law Administrators. Got a lemon and can't get help? Try this Web site.

CHARITIES

http://www.give.org. It's a good idea to investigate a charity before you start shelling out dollars. The Better Business Bureau's Wise Giving Alliance lists several hundred legitimate national charities. Check its Web site or call 1-703-276-0100. This resource is for national charities only, like Red Cross or United Way. It will not list local charities such as a food drive sponsored by your church. If you're still unsure, ask Clark Howard's staff at 1-404-872-0750 between the hours of 1:00 p.m to 4:00 p.m. EST or call toll-free 1-877-87-CLARK (only for those outside the Atlanta area).

CREDIT COUNSELING

http://www.nfcc.org. The National Foundation for Credit Counseling will provide you with a list of credit counselors nationwide. Call toll-free at 1-800-388-2227.

http://www.consumercredit.com. American Consumer Credit Counseling helps seniors with debt problems. Visit its Web site or call toll-free 1-800-769-3571.

IDENTITY THEFT

For an annual credit report call the following credit rating agencies:

Equifax 1-800-685-1111 (**http://www.equifax.com**)

Experian 1-888-397-3742 (**http://www.experian.com**)

TransUnion 1-800-888-4213 (**http://www.transunion.com**)

http://www.PrivacyGuard.com. If you'd like one firm to alert you (for a fee) when someone applies for credit in your name, visit PrivacyGuard online or call toll-free 1-877-202-8828.

http://www.idtheftcenter.org/index.shtml. The Identity Theft Resource Center has a trove of information that will help you identify scams and prevent identity theft.

1-888-567-8688. Consumer reporting industry's opt-out telephone number. Call this number toll-free to opt out of marketing promotions from companies issuing credit cards and selling insurance.

http://surfshield.net. Consider using an anonymous surfer such as Surf Net that allows you to surf the Internet without leaving an identification trail. There are many such services on the Internet, some commercial, others free. Surf Net is a freebee.

INSURANCE

http://www.ambest.com. A.M. Best is the recognized authority on rating insurance companies. Use its Web site to check your prospective insurer and learn useful information about the insurance industry that will help you prevent scams.

http://www.insurancefraud.org. The Coalition Against Insurance Fraud educates the public about insurance fraud. It also refers consumers to appropriate agencies to report a scam and get help. Call 1-202-393-7330.

http://www.naic.org/cis/index.00. The National Association of Insurance Commissioners lists problems consumers have had with different insurers. The Web site contains much useful information, including addresses and telephone numbers for the insurance commissions in every state.

INVESTMENTS

http://www.nasaa.org. The Web site of North American Securities Administrators Association (NASAA). Every investor should be required to work through the investor education section of this terrific Web site before investing a dollar. The site also exposes investor scams, some of them remarkably sophisticated.

http://sec.gov/investor/brokers.htm. The Securities and Exchange Commission (SEC) maintains a database that shows disciplinary actions taken against brokers and financial advisors. Check here first to make sure your financial advisor is not on the list before you allow him or her to counsel you.

LEGAL AID

http://www.abanet.org/legalservices/probono/directory.html. The American Bar Association publishes a Directory of Pro Bono Programs by state for seniors who can ill afford expensive legal services. The Web site also explains how an individual qualifies for legal advice donated by attorneys. If that doesn't get you the kind of inexpensive legal advice you need, try one of the two Web sites listed here:

http://www.nlada.org. The National Legal Aid & Defender Association.
http://www.lsc.gov. The Legal Services Corporation.

LIVING WILLS

http://www.uslivingwillregistry.com/forms.shtm. Assuming you do not want to use a lawyer to establish your living will (I personally advise that you *always* use a lawyer to construct or review any legal contract) and have no interest in a durable power of attorney for health care, you can download a living will form for your state from the U.S. Living Will Registry.

MUTUAL FUNDS

http://www.Morningstar.com. Morningstar is the most recognized rating organization for mutual funds and the standard for the mutual fund industry. Use it to check the rating of the mutual fund your financial advisor recommends. And whatever else you do, read the annual mutual fund issue of *Consumer Reports* for its mutual fund recommendations.

NURSING HOMES

http://www.consumeraffairs.com/news_index/nursing_home.html. For an eye-opener regarding nursing home atrocities, and why you should think twice before committing a relative, read the stories at this Web site.

http://www.medicare.gov. If you're still adamant about using a nursing home, go to the Medicare Web site (operated by the U.S. Department of Health and Human Services) and click on its Nursing Home Compare link to find out how the nursing home you're considering rates. This is an invaluable service provided free by the government.

http://www.eldercare.gov. Another excellent service of the U.S. Department of Health and Human Services that helps the elderly locate local and state support services. Visit its Web site or call toll-free 1-800-677-1116.

PHARMACIES

http://www.overseaspharmacy.com. Thinking of ordering drugs from overseas? Then check this Web site for starters. Keep in mind that the FDA forbids the importation of drugs.

http://CRBestBuyDrugs.org. *Consumer Reports* has an online service devoted to advising you on the cheapest and safest drugs available, including a list of generic drugs.

http://www.nabp.net. The National Association of Boards of Pharmacy will let you know whether an online pharmacy is licensed and in good standing. Visit the Web site or call 1-847-698-6227.

http://www.pharmacychecker.com. When purchasing drugs from Canada, check this Web site first to see if the pharmacy of your choice is certified by the Canadian International Pharmacy Association (CIPA).

PC (HARD DRIVE) FIREWALL PROTECTION

http://www.pcmag.com. Go to *PC* magazine's Web site's download section and type in "Zone Alarm firewall." Then follow download instructions. This free firewall will protect you against many (but not all) hacker intrusions.

As alternatives, you can also download both free and commercial firewalls from:
PC World at http://www.pcworld.com/downloads.
ZD Net at http://downloads-zdnet.com.

POSTAL FRAUD

http://www.usps.com/postalinspectors. Report any suspected cases of postal fraud either online or at your local post office.

TAX FRAUD

If you suspect you've been defrauded by scammers impersonating IRS agents, call the Treasury Inspector General's hotline at 1-800-366-4484.

TELEMARKETING

http://www.donotcall.gov. The national Do-Not-Call Registry. Listing your name and telephone number here will exempt you from many nuisance telemarketing intrusions for a period of five years, after which you need to renew.

http://www.fraud.org/aaft/aaftinfo.htm. The National Consumers League Alliance Against Fraud in Telemarketing and Electronic Commerce. Call 1-202-835-3323. Educates the public about telemarketing fraud and online fraud. This Web site, chock full of useful information, shows seniors how to shop safely online.

TRAVEL PLANS (CHARTERS)

If you're suspicious about the legitimacy of a charter operator's name and address, check with the U.S. Department of Transportation (DOT), Aviation Consumer Protection Division in Washington DC by calling 1-202-366-2220. It could save you a pile of money.

WORK-AT-HOME SCHEMES

http://www.workathomesourcebook.com. *The Work at Home Sourcebook* should be your first stop before you decide to work at home. It can help you prevent costly mistakes since many work-at-home offers are outright scams and many more provide marginal income.

Just a word about additional research. The Internet contains literally thousands of valuable resources to help seniors discover how to combat scams. The few I have listed will at least start you out. The rest is up to you. Happy hunting.

Index

dangerous spam e-mail, 105–9
  preventing, 106–9
  spotting, 105–6
debit cards, 28–30
debt-management services. *See* credit counseling services
deed stripping, 123
deliveries, phony package, 53–54, 56
dial-up Internet connections, 22
dieticians, 92
diet scams, 90–92
disposal of financial documents, 19, 34
disputing charges, 28–29
doctors
  approval before starting exercise programs, 68
  Medicare fraud and, 80–82
documents, disposal of, 19, 34
Do-Not-Call Registry, 201–3
  resources, 247
door-to-door salesmen scams, 176–79
  preventing, 177–79
  spotting, 177
Double Indemnity (movie), 96
double-team sales tactics, 229–30
downloads (downloading) from Web sites, 23
drug plans, Medicare, 77–79
drugs, online pharmacies, 86–89, 246
durable power of attorney, 73

electronic card-swipe devices, 13, 14
electronic scanner errors, 191–93
e-mail accounts, free, 105, 106–7
e-mail attachments, 108
e-mail check alerts, 17
e-mail spam, 105–9
  preventing, 106–9
  spotting, 105–6
endorsement of checks, 19

Equifax, 33–34, 242
equity stripping, 121–22
event tickets, fake, 168–70
executive (career) marketing scams, 212–15
Experian, 33–34, 242
eye surgery, laser, 69–71

fake auto accidents, 48–50
fake charities, 156–58
fake event tickets, 168–70
fake IRS letters, 128–29
fake Meals on Wheels, 51–52
fake package deliveries, 53–54, 56
fake police, 57–59
fake senior services, 51–52
Federal Communications Commission (FCC), 200, 238
Federal Trade Commission (FTC), 238
  Cooling-Off Rule, 179
  credit counseling, 26
  Do-Not-Call Registry, 201–3, 247
  lotteries and sweepstakes, 164
  phishing, 112
fees
  for credit counselors, 25, 26
  for health clubs, 66, 67, 68
  for mutual funds, 133–35
financial planners, 114–16
financial seminars, 117–20
firewalls, for computer, 23, 246
fitness club scams, 66–68
fixed annuities, 142
flight insurance, 95
flipping loans, 122–23
foreign lotteries and sweepstakes, 162–64
fortune-teller cons, 54, 56
franchises, 216–18
Fraud.com, 205, 237
Fraud Hotline of Health and Human Services, 78, 245